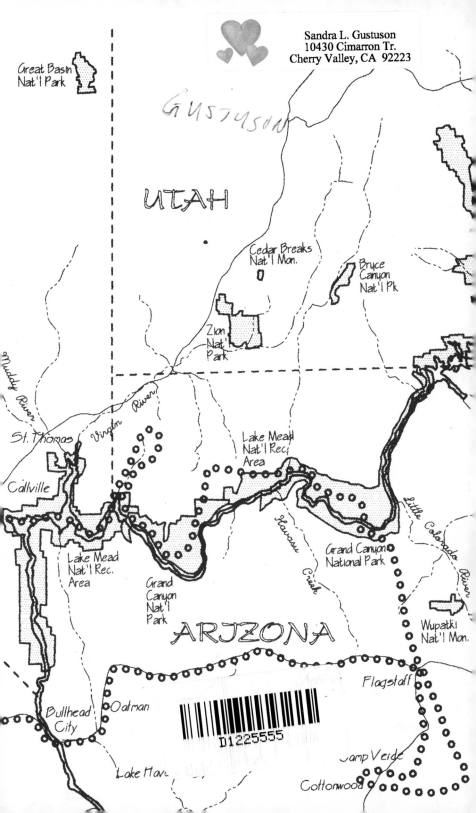

Great Basin
Nat'l Park

Sandra L. Gustuson
10430 Cimarron Tr.
Cherry Valley, CA 92223

GUSTUSON

UTAH

Cedar Breaks
Nat'l Mon.

Bryce
Canyon
Nat'l Pk

Zion
Nat'l
Park

Muddy River

Virgin River

St. Thomas

Lake Mead
Nat'l Rec.
Area

Callville

Little Colorado River

Havasu Creek

Grand Canyon
National Park

Lake Mead
Nat'l Rec.
Area

Grand
Canyon
Nat'l
Park

ARIZONA

Wupatki
Nat'l Mon.

Flagstaff

Bullhead
City

Oatman

D1225555

Camp Verde

Lake Hav...

Cottonwood

DEATH VALLEY NATURAL HISTORY ASSOCIATION
is a non-profit organization pledged to aid the National Park
Service in the preservation and interpretation of
Death Valley National Monument.

Photos credits as acknowledged. The remainder from author's
family album. Captions developed from author's comments
on the backs of the photographs.
Author's photographs reproduced by the courtesy of
William L. Price, Jr.

Map—Doug Madsen

Text from
the 1973 edition.
Death Valley Natural History
Association added photos
and captions.

This book was represented for
sale to the publisher by the
literary agency of
Alive Communications,
P.O. Box 49068,
Colorado Springs, CO 80949.

"Burro Bill" Price

Burro Bill and Me

Edna Calkins Price

Copyright 1984, 1993
Luther S. and Marilyn H. Weare

Library of Congress Card Number 72-97363

ISBN: 1-878900-28-5

Published 1993
by the
Death Valley
Natural History Association
P.O. Box 188
Death Valley, CA 92328

This book is published in cooperation
with
The National Park Service
by the
Death Valley Natural History Association

TO BILL JUNIOR

Every story should have such a happy ending.

ABOUT THIS EDITION

In 1972 I achieved every newspaperman's dream when I purchased a weekly newspaper in Idyllwild, a small village 5,200 feet up in the San Jacinto Mountains of Southern California.

As a newcomer, while I moved around town I kept running into an elderly woman, Edna Price, who was sort of an icon in the village. Earlier, in the days before there was a resident physician in Idyllwild, Edna had kept people patched up. In her youth she had been a trained nurse. In the 1950s and '60s in Idyllwild she functioned as a kind of paramedic before there were such people. Doctors off the Hill kept her supplied with drugs and in her kindly way she did what she could for friends and neighbors. If someone was seriously ill, she sent him or her elsewhere for care. She was not above donning snowshoes and accompanying rescue teams when someone was injured in the wilderness in winter. People simply worshiped this good woman.

Edna had a history. As a refined young Virginia girl she had somehow crossed paths with a semiliterate ex-circus roustabout with the soul of an adventurer. He was a magnetic fellow and it was love at first sight.

Married life eventually took the couple to the scorching wasteland of Death Valley and the Arizona badlands. For ten years (1931 to 1941) Edna and Bill happily slept under the stars. By day they scratched an existence from the barren desert and hobnobbed with prospectors, outlaws and adventurers. They were doing in the 1930s what so many young people sought to do years later: they had abandoned the urban rat race and found peace close to nature.

It was a great story, and in fact years before I met her, Edna had written about it. She urged me to read her "book." Finally, one day after the Town Crier had gone to press I took an afternoon off and read the manuscript.

I was amazed. It was a jewel of Western Americana in my judgment, an absorbing story written in simple, lucid prose, full of colorful characterizations and reflecting Edna's wholesome gaiety. The contrast between her sedate background and the harsh life in the desert was vividly presented. It was what is nowadays described as a "good read" and I determined to publish it. I ordered 2,000 copies printed to sell locally.

Edna gloried in the touch of fame the book brought her and the pride her family showed in her achievement.

Edna died the following year, but "Burro Bill and Me" lives on. Although the book was out of print for many years, requests for copies kept arriving. It was obvious that "Burro Bill and Me" deserved wider circulation.

Discovering the book and bringing it to print originally was an exciting experience. I am happy that this new edition by the Death Valley Natural History Association will enable a larger public to enjoy Mrs. Price's rich, fun-filled narrative.

One footnote is appropriate: Although Edna and Burro Bill continued to enjoy their unique lifestyle, in 1941 they made their move away from Death Valley. The reason: Edna was pregnant. Hence the dedication of this book.

Luther Weare

Idyllwild, California
1993

The Prices traveled around the Sand Dunes, over
Daylight Pass to reach Beatty, Nevada.
—NPS photo

BAKER,
CALIFORNIA
1941

On the shaded porch of Failing's Cafe, a handful of wilted travelers glanced anxiously toward heat waves dancing over desert sands, then back to the porch thermometer, and up the long shimmering grade toward Las Vegas, Nevada. Lounging on cement steps at their feet, indolent natives of the desert outpost idly waited for darkness, with its cool promise of renewed life.

"God," groaned a traveling salesman, "What a country! I keep thinking of those old-time prospectors, prodding their burros up that scorching grade. Ever see any of those old fellows around here?"

"Sure," replied a miner, poking at my husband with a grubby forefinger, "Him."

"Him?" cried the salesman incredulously, sweeping Bill's smooth face, trim jeans and neat boots with a scornful stare.

BURRO BILL AND ME

"Why he's just a tenderfoot! You ought to see the old couple I saw one time."

He mopped his red perspiring face. "It was on a lonesome stretch of desert," he continued, "in the damnedest howling sandstorm this side of Hell. A wall of flying sand hit me and I pulled my car off the road to let it clear a bit. All of a sudden this couple popped out of the storm and headed out across the desert. They were bent over double, facing into the teeth of that wind, but I got a good look as they passed by. The old man was a sight—big bushy red beard, long hair way down on his shoulders—looked like pictures of Buffalo Bill. And he had the skinniest legs in the tightest old Levis. But that old woman!"

He looked around at his eager listeners. "That old woman," he proclaimed reverently, "She was a real old pioneer, tough, and weathered and hard as nails. She was bringing up the rear, booting two pack burros in the rump, and cussing a blue streak. Now those," he concluded triumphantly, "those were *REAL* desert rats!"

Bill caught my eye and shook his head warningly. I was choking with silent laughter at this pithy but accurate description of myself and Bill during those years when we knew no bed but the ground, no roof but the sky, when we were known all over the deserts simply as Burro Bill and Mrs. Bill.

Looking back now, I could scarcely believe the bewildering array of adventures that had befallen us since that spring day ten years before, when Bill had revolted against a life of ease and deliberately tossed aside material comforts for the toughest existence left in America—that of foot travelers in the wastelands of the West.

WILLIE HATED COMFORT

When Bill was fourteen, down in Arkansas, he had tossed his school books under the wheels of a slow-moving freight and caught the rods on his first adventure. After that, not even his mother's tears could still in his heart that nameless longing awakened by the long low mourn of a freight train whistling in the night.

He became a migrant worker—a "stiff" he called it—and worked his way all over the United States and into the fields of Canadian wheat. He became in turn a harvest hand, a logger, a miner, a section hand, a jack of all trades. I met him on one of his periodic visits to Little Rock where I was nursing in a government hospital. He was a gay and cocky youth of 23, and I a sedate young woman of 26, but it was love at first sight. In three months we were married and to my family in Virginia I wrote rather hazy details, fearing they would not exactly approve of a migrant "stiff" for a son-in-law.

BURRO BILL AND ME

For the next five years we moved, always finding work, but always living in cheap rooms, in dingy neighborhoods—in St. Louis, Chicago, Kansas City. Bill worked in hospitals, too. He was called an attendant, his main job being in psychopathic wards or on ambulances. In Kansas City he registered for private cases and soon was called to the bedside of one of the nation's leading millionaires. Soon I was also added to the family menage, and in a private car attached to fast mail trains we saw America.

At first it was fun. When you've ridden the rods, it is only natural to revel in the luxury of special cars with division-superintendents bowing you in and out, and schedules arranged for your convenience. We settled for the winter in Coronado, one of California's most exclusive resorts.

Bill soon grew bored, and longed for the freedom that had once been his. One day we crossed a bridge near La Jolla, and saw a group of "jungle bums" cooking a pot of stew down below. Bill tossed a silver dollar to the seedy men and sighed, "I envy them— they are *free*."

Then one day he announced bluntly, "I can't take this soft life. It rots a man. If it weren't for you—Say," he interrupted himself eagerly, "what do you say we quit this job? Buy a camp outfit? Just keep going till our money plays out?"

It had come at last! Bill's mother had warned me. "You'd best keep your hat in your hand, girl," she whispered to me. "That Willie of mine won't wait till you can get it off a nail. He just don't like comfort."

I stared at Bill. "And what will we do when the money is gone?" I asked.

WILLIE HATED COMFORT

"We'll worry about that when the time comes," Bill assured me confidently. "Nobody ever starved to death in America. But," he added as an afterthought, "we may get damned hungry sometimes!"

Sand Dunes, Death Valley National Monument
—NPS photo

Fremont Street, Las Vegas, Nevada. Early 1930s.
—Logan Collection, UNLV

WE CHOOSE THE WASTELANDS

Having no idea which way to start on such an aimless adventure, we sent for a sheaf of illustrated travel folders. One by one, Bill studied them intently, discarding them with a "too civilized—too many people—phony" until he came to one that struck his fancy.

Death Valley, the folder proclaimed, was a desolate narrow white sink, hemmed in by forbidding tumbled ranges. Emigrants crossing its barren wastes had died without food or water, for in this valley of death nothing was believed to grow. Burro-prospectors too, in their search for gold, had strewn it with their bleaching bones. Today, it could be entered by car over rugged desert roads, but only during the winter and early spring months. It was one of the most primitive areas accessible to tourists in the entire United States.

That was enough for Bill. We bought our camp outfit and, ignoring the calendar, were soon on our way. Three days later we reached the western slope of the Panamint Range.

On the steep grade leading into Wild Rose Canyon, we steamed to a stop, puzzled by the sudden appearance on this desolate roadside of a shiny five gallon can obviously placed with care. Propped against it was a crudely lettered sign, "WATER. HELP YOURSELF AND BRING THE CAN TO THE NEXT WATER, 3 MILES." We filled our boiling radiator and carried the can on to Wild Rose Spring.

From a cabin on the canyon's edge came a stooped man of about sixty, with faded quizzical blue eyes and a drooping tobacco-yellowed mustache. "Well, see you found your water all right," he remarked pleasantly, reaching for the empty can. "Always keep some on that grade for tenderfeet that don't know 'nuf to put a car in low gear and take it easy. They all gun their cars when the goin' gets tough, and by the time they hit the worst grade, most of 'em have boiled plumb dry. Seems a shame for folks to hike three miles, so I always keep some water down there by the road."

"But doesn't anyone ever take your cans?" we asked.

"Why no," he replied simply. "It says right on the sign to bring 'em here."

Mac put us up for the night in an empty cabin across the narrow canyon from his own, and bustled hospitably around bringing us an armful of wood for our stove and filling our canteens from the spring. "Put a few layers of gunny-sack around the canteens," advised Mac. "Keep the sacks wet and the water stays cool even on hot days. That desert water bag you got is fine for camp but on the road, just when you need it worst, the damn thing will spring a leak and leave you to choke to death. Don't trust your water to a cloth bag—water's worth its weight in gold on this desert."

I was learning. "They say people die in Death Valley with full canteens," I volunteered. "Why is that?"

"I don't know," admitted Mac, "and nobody else seems to. Myself, I think there must be a sort of a poisonous miasma that rises from the ground, mostly in summer. I've lived on the edge of that Valley for six years and I ain't been down in it yet. Don't aim to either."

"Well, we came to see Death Valley," said Bill undismayed. "They say tourists are beginning to go in there, as many as six or eight cars in one day. It can't be so bad if tourists can get through."

"Yeah, they go in till April fifteenth," protested Mac. "It's May now and hot as the hinges of Hell. Better stay here with me awhile, and then go back the way you come."

For three days we roamed the sun-scorched hills, poking into long-dead mining camps. At night we sat with Mac in the dim lamp-light of his cabin while he brought from his memory adventures of the old burro-men. Once he interrupted himself to knock sharply on the wall and out scampered two mice. Mac spoke to them gently, fed them from his hand and to our astonishment left them to romp fearlessly with his old gray cat.

"Training 'em passes away a lot of time," smiled Mac. "Sometimes in summer nobody comes by for two-three weeks." Yet the old prospector, in his solitude, seemed deeply content.

When we left for Death Valley he shook our hands warmly

saying, "If you ever decide to settle down, come back here. We make beans all right."

If the hardy traveler survived Eichbaum's toll road, the next hazard was his hotel caretaker, old John, the self-styled "Duke of Luxembourg." He had the road blocked with a heavy chain. We honked and he came out scowling fiercely, a heavy mattock in one hand.

"Vat you vant?" he demanded.

"We want to go through," replied Bill.

"It's closed—no more tourists," growled old John, hefting the mattock a bit suggestively.

"Oh well," said Bill lightly, "it doesn't matter. We just wanted to see your beautiful little resort. Did you do all that rock work? Why, you're a real artist."

Old John melted. "Come inside," he grunted. "You see something much better. All this I do—and this—yes, the Duke of Luxembourg is an artist. Come. Maybe you like a little vine and some lunch with me?"

John was lonely and garrulous, and we spent several hours listening to his fierce lambasting of his fellow man. Then we got into our car and began turning around.

"Hey, where you going?" cried John. "I thought you vant to go this way," and jerking the chain from its post, he motioned us out, around his seven-room hotel, and across the Valley. Bill winked at me as we waved goodbye.

A short way out we came to the great dunes of Death Valley and promptly got stuck in the sand. Nowhere could we see anything to put under our wheels, until Bill walked out and found an old movie location, almost buried in the dunes. He called me to help him carry a plank to the car. There was a loaf of rye bread, perfect in appearance as the day it was baked, lying on the dunes, but when I touched it, it fell into powder. A few old shoes lying about were hard and curled, shriveled to one-fourth their original size. The plank was heavy, the heat intolerable, and the trip back supreme effort. Deep sands tugged at our feet; our bones were jello. When we reached the car we guzzled water eagerly while clouds of huge horseflies swarmed on the drops spilled from our lips. Just thirteen miles out of Stovepipe we discovered that between us we had drunk two gallons of water. As fast as we poured it in, the fiery dry air sucked it from our pores.

Farther down the Valley we saw our first mirage, a blue lake beckoning, never nearer, with reedy shores where tiny rowboats bobbed gently at a long pier. Just before we reached Furnace Creek it melted away and all that remained was a burning white alkali flat over which heat waves danced dizzily.

At Furnace Creek camp we took showers and found ourselves dry before we could reach for a towel. An army blanket, thoroughly saturated, dried in only ten minutes. Death Valley in May was a great blast furnace, searing, shriveling, destructive. Yet— that infinite arching sky, the brooding purple mountains, the symphony of blended color, the solitude and peace of its empty wastes—these were things we would always remember. "When it's cooler," said Bill musingly, "I'd like to come back to this country."

In 1931, Bill drove this road from Salt Creek to Beatty to buy supplies. 1931.

Salt Creek Trading Post set up at the site of the last camp of the Jayhawkers. Mineral specimens, bottles colored purple by the sun, tools abandoned by the prospectors, Indian relics, but especially Jack the burro enticed tourists to stop at Salt Creek Crossing. January 1931.

SQUATTERS ON THE RIGHT-OF-WAY

Climbing out of the blinding heat, we turned our Ford toward the cool snow-capped Sierras. Living for each day alone, we roamed their roads, pausing for days or weeks at a time to fish, to climb a glacier; once to help a stump-rancher put up his hay when we found him with an infected hand which we lanced and treated.

Gradually discarding non-essentials, we learned to camp. First we sent home the trunk and suitcases that I had insisted on bringing, "just in case" we needed some good clothes. We gave away the huge umbrella tent we had chosen for its roominess and in its place we bought a tiny explorers' tent weighing but seven pounds. Next to go was the steel folding bed that required so much time to set up and refold each day, besides almost freezing us to death with the cold wind blowing underneath. Sleeping on a springy bed of boughs or brush was far more comfortable. Last to go were our camp chairs and folding table, and from then on life was simple and complete.

But with the first fall winds nipping through our light clothing, it was time to make plans for the future. Our funds were running low.

"Remember the old fellow Mac, in Wild Rose Canyon?" asked Bill. "He said if we ever decided to settle down to come back—we could make beans on the desert. I liked that desert. It sort of gets a man. Let's go back to Mac and that little empty cabin we slept in before."

Our hearts sang with eagerness as we again drove up to the site of Mac's water cans. . . . There were none. On to Wild Rose. Another old man in Mac's cabin. Mac had a new cabin a mile above, he said. We went on. There was the same kindly Mac, but no look of recognition lit his face. We had come back to him and he did not remember us!

"So many new people now," he said sadly, "so many new faces—. But," he added kindly, "there's a good cabin back at the spring. You jes' stay anyway."

"What happened to your water cans, Mac?"

"Oh," he sighed, "tourists began comin' and they kept takin' 'em. Cost me forty cents apiece. Guess folks have to pack their own water these days."

As we turned to go, our eyes fastened on a slip of brown paper tacked to his door. Mac's cabin had stood always open, unquestioning, to the traveler. Now the slip read, "HELP YOURSELF—BUT WASH THE DISHES!" Yes, the tourists had come.

We found our little cabin still vacant, perched on its rocky cliff just below the spring. "Who owns it?" I asked.

SQUATTERS ON THE RIGHT-OF-WAY

"No one," replied Mac serenely. "These desert cabins are generally built on mining claims and if the owner lets his claim go he loses the cabin when he moves out. This one happens to be built on the highway right-of-way and you have as much right to it as anyone else."

And so we moved into the cabin that was to be our home. It was of rough clean boards, bare rafters above, plank floor beneath. There were two rooms, clean and airy but bare of furniture save for two army cots, a huge wood range (in this woodless canyon) and a plank table and bench. Outside we found a desert cooler—a board cupboard covered with burlap, over which was suspended a five-gallon can for water. From holes punched in the bottom of the can, cloth wicks dribbled the water evenly over the burlap sacking, cooling the cupboard by rapid evaporation. Even in mid-summer, Mac told us, butter did not melt nor canned milk sour.

Strangers to the desert usually think of it as an endless expanse of shifting dunes, void of life and vegetation. Gradually, we learned that the desert is a panorama of change, of fleeting mood and color, where wrinkled purple ranges frown on burning white alkali valleys. In the canyons spring little green oases, where clear water trickles through desert willows and disappears in sandy soil. Had the ill-fated forty-niners only known that in Death Valley one climbs for his water—that in nearly every canyon of the rugged old Panamint Range were clear cool springs!

Wild Rose Canyon boasted five springs, where lived our neighbors, the prospectors and Indians. High on the slopes above were the summer camps of the Panamint Indians, close to their fall harvest of pinon nuts and their hunting grounds for the big-horn

15

sheep. In winter, they moved down to Death Valley to harvest their staple food, the nutritious bean of the thorny mesquite.

Farther down, where the canyon gathered itself into narrower confines of sage and willow, was the tiny tumble-down shack of Shorty Harris, the declining "Dean of Desert Rats," and past him a half-mile or so stood Mac's neat little gray cabin, newly built of lumber salvaged from deserted mining camps.

Then where the canyon finally pinched and squeezed between high rocky walls, bubbled our little spring. Sitting on opposite sides of the gorge, two cabins stared each other in the face, ours and that of Old Dan Driscoll. Past us straggled all the in-coming and out-going settlers as well as some few tourists who wished to avoid the three-dollar toll on the Eichbaum road to Death Valley. On our road to Death Valley lived Neighbor George, Shorty Borden, Jack Stewart and Bill Corcoran—our "fur neighbors," Mac called them.

As soon as they heard of the new people in the country, they came—from shacks, from tents and hillside caves, bouncing and rattling over the dirt roads in ancient Fords, Willyses, Franklins, and even one chain-driven Maxwell. In these cars they carried a few canned goods, an axe, shovel, pick, and gold-pan, twenty gallons of water, a spare can of gas, and a huge bed-roll wrapped in canvas. Having their entire belongings with them, there never seemed much point in returning to mere shelter, so their visits sometimes stretched into days, even weeks if times were a bit hard.

"Share and share alike—that's our motto," declared Neighbor George, on his first visit. "What's yours is mine—what's mine is yours," he added expansively, studying our well-filled grocery shelf with a hungry eye.

"Jack Stewart, an old prospector at his cabin in Darwin where we stayed. I'm really not thumbing my nose, I happened to laugh. Notice the ice box on the side of the house, gunny sack patented. You will also see how convenient it is to dump the tin cans."

"I had a boyish haircut for our burro trip only, but it did make me look lean and lank beside Gladys. She said I look like Mum in her lean *days. If she lived off the country, she'd be lean, too." Received August 12, 1931.*

GEORGE

George, it developed, knew nothing of prospecting. He had been left behind as a watchman, by a lead mine, long since defunct. After two years with no word from his employers, George had appropriated the mine in lieu of wages. Every so often he sold a piece of machinery and lived for a time in style. Between sales, he just borrowed, augmenting his borrowings with wild burro meat, which he consumed two pounds to a sitting. All the prospectors kept their burros well out of George's district, for he could never look at one without mentally skinning it out.

After George had borrowed a few cans of milk and a pound of coffee, he asked Bill to ride to Trona with him. Bill wisely carried only seven dollars which George promptly borrowed to buy a hundred pounds of ice and a beer strainer. Then they backtracked and headed for Darwin, where George borrowed enough credit at the general store to bring home coconut, cake coloring and marshmallow whip.

BURRO BILL AND ME

For our seven dollars we got two fluted patty shells, filled with messy fruit salad, topped with marshmallow whip, and dribbled over with green and pink icing. George carried them the ten miles from his home in Wood Canyon, unwrapped, carefully balanced on one moist dirty paw, and held them out with pride and joy.

"For you," he grinned, exposing a row of broken brown snags. "One for Bill, too. Eat them right now, while they're nice and fresh." He spit tobacco juice out the door and admired his masterpiece at length.

"Oh, no," I gulped, "they're too pretty to eat—*how* did you do it?"

"It's nothing," disclaimed George modestly. "Now when I was head chef at the Waldorf-Astoria—"

I stuffed the concoction into my mouth, and swallowed fast. Bill stuffed his into his shirt front and ran to the back door, but George was happily describing a fanciful job among the Waldorf pastries, and did not notice.

Once George borrowed money from Mac and sent to Sears Roebuck for a bread mixer, an ice-cream freezer, a canning outfit and a case of tin cans. Having nothing to can, he also ordered a wooden box each of dried apricots and prunes, which he stewed, canned and pasted neatly with typewritten labels. For his twenty dollars, Mac was happy to receive a shiny tin can, labeled "Apricot Jelly—Made and Canned by George G—May 30, 1931, Argenta, Cal." Argenta was the mythical name of the mythical city in which George lived. (Argenta, I recalled, is Latin for silver.)

Between George and Mac there was a firm friendship, strengthened by repeated misunderstandings. Once Mac went away to work, leaving his cabin unlocked as usual. George hied himself over and "borrowed" Mac's precious canned ham that always stood on the pantry shelf, inviolate, a symbol of affluence for all to see. He also took along a case of Mac's potent home-brew.

When Mac returned, he stopped off to have a chat with George before going to his own cabin, and was mildly surprised that the impecunious George was able to offer him a nice thick ham sandwich and a bottle of beer. When he found he was eating his own ham and drinking his own beer, retribution was swift. He finished off the beer, got rip-snorting drunk, backed his old Overland into George's tarpaper shack, leaving a huge new opening, and stormed off. Since they were even, all was forgiven and for Christmas Mac made George a fresh batch of brew, and George borrowed some money from Mac and sent to Sears for a little white porcelain sink which he beamingly presented to the overcome lender.

George was a whiz at anything mechanical and kept everything running, from our old clocks to our old cars. But just ask him a question and George was good for at least an hour of long and detailed explanation during which he never took his pale pinpoint eyes from one's face, so that the questioner had no choice but to stare right back. It was a wearing mode of conversation, and Bill was always champing to get his word in too. Once he interrupted in an attempt to sidetrack George with the irrelevant query, "George, how far do you call it from your place to ours?" George halted and considered.

"I don't know," he announced at last.

" 'Bout ten miles would you say?" persisted Bill.

"Well, now," replied George with the air of weighing a momentous bit of information, "I measured it at least ten times, and it never came out the same. It varies anywhere from nine and nine-tenths to nine and eight-tenths. So, I can't rightly say that I know how far it is." That was George, with a head for mathematics.

George lived in a dry camp. He figured the cost of his water at seven dollars a gallon, which included his time at mechanic's wages, wear and tear on his car, cost of gasoline, even the wear and tear on the cans and canteens in which it was carried from our spring to his cabin. Naturally, at this price, George wasted no water on washing.

Figuring was his daytime amusement. At night he just lay on his bunk and stared at the ceiling or at nude ladies cut from the pages of the Police Gazette, that adorned his walls. Pinned to his dirty striped flannel pajamas was the deputy sheriff's badge that he wore on his shirt by day, for George was our self-styled "law." He had secured the badge and permit to carry a gun while he was watchman for the mine, and he at once assumed the role of local officer of the law and self-appointed aide to J. Edgar Hoover. Not a car passed by night that escaped George's eager ear, and many were the innocent tourists that George suspected of "rum-running" or "dope peddling." Respectable folks should travel by day or at least make a courtesy call on the arm of the law, opined George, suggestively fingering the old forty-five that he still wore in the seclusion of his own canyon. Sometimes I wished that the sheriff's office would wake up and revoke the permit and badge,

GEORGE

apparently long since forgotten, in this vast backwash that was
Inyo County.

*"How do you like our child? He's a darling—eats my toast right out of my hand
each A.M. with his forefeet planted in the kitchen, and his hind feet outdoors. He's
Bill's chief delight. Edna." February 12, 1931*

"A drink for everyone from a desert stream under Mt. Whitney near Lone Pine, California."

JACK STEWART AND BILL CORCORAN

Bill Corcoran was a former burro-man, powerful, nearing fifty, with a face much like Jack Dempsey's. He had a voice that was pure music, and it rang in the ears like a deep-toned bell as he told his famous stories so cleverly that it was impossible to tell where fact gave way to fancy.

Between Corcoran and his partner, Jack Stewart, there was a strong bond of affection mixed with mutual exasperation. Their arguments were fierce and blighting. Once they quarreled over a box of chocolate creams that Corcoran had brought home. Every day a few chocolates were missing and Corcoran became secretly suspicious and then openly accusing.

"I didn't steal your blasted old chocolates," protested Jack over and over, but still the chocolates continued to vanish. Bitterness and hostility grew until the partners refused to speak.

BURRO BILL AND ME

For days this silence wore upon their leashed tempers until Corcoran could stand it no longer and he prepared to set out for Lone Pine. He buttoned himself into a clean shirt and reached under his bunk for his "town" shoes. Staring absently before him, he thrust in one foot—and felt a soft sticky mass ooze through his toes. He swallowed hard and looked. There, squashing through the eyelets, over the shoe top and out onto the dirt floor were his missing chocolate creams. Pack rats had done the deed. The reconciliation that followed was touching.

Most of the things that befell Jack Stewart and Bill Corcoran were results of their thirst. Corcoran had a prodigious capacity for "raw red likker." Once he had a frightening case of "the snakes."

"The doc in Lone Pine," said Corcoran, "advised me to give up likker. I told him I just had to have a drink before I could get up in the morning and he says for me to eat an apple a day. 'When you want to drink,' he says, 'just reach for an apple.' So I brings me home a box of Olancha Valley apples and lay one out on the table between the bunks so's I can reach for it as soon as I open my eyes.

"Well, next morning I was awake afore daylight, and did I ever need a drink! In the dark, I reaches out for my apple and takes a big bite. I let out a yowl and threw the damn thing clean out the tent door—it tasted just like punky wood. Jeez, I thought, them's the damnedest apples I ever et—or is it *me*? Anyway, I pulled up the covers and laid there with the shakes till daylight and then I went out to rinse that wooden taste out of my mouth. I looked everywhere for that lousy apple. I didn't find it, but do you know what I picked up offen the ground right outside my tent door? A damn old dried-up burro dropping with one whole side bit off of it! Them damn pack rats traded me while I was asleep!"

One tale that Bill Corcoran loved to tell to open-mouthed tourists involved a certain trip to Lone Pine for supplies. In Lone Pine, he had imbibed freely of "raw corn likker" and carried along a jug to keep him company across the eighty-mile stretch home. Driving along the newly paved road between Lone Pine and Olancha, he suddenly became aware of a smooth silence, quite unlike the accustomed rattle and bang of his ancient Model-T.

"Hell, it's stopped," thought Corcoran and stepped out to see what was the matter. To his astonishment he sprawled flat on his face and the car hurtled off the road and came to rest against a telephone pole, the wheels spinning crazily in mid-air. Just then a man drove up and stopped. "My God, man!" he exclaimed, "I was going forty miles an hour and I couldn't begin to keep up with you."

"Hum," muttered Corcoran, "I must be drunker than I thought." He retrieved the car and set forth. Soon he passed an old tramp miner hiking wearily along the road. He pulled to a stop and backed up.

"Get in," he called. "Where you headed?"

"Oh, no place in particular," replied the man vaguely, "Just goin'."

"Well, then," urged Corcoran hospitably, "you just as well come go home with me and I'll bring you back next trip in."

His new-found friend accepted gratefully. "That's mighty kind of you and I don't mind if I do."

"Have a drink on it," said Corcoran, proffering his jug. The miner swigged a long deep swig and Corcoran took another. They came to Olancha and it was cold. "Let's have one to warm up on," suggested Corcoran.

Leaving the pavement at Olancha, the Ford fell into its familiar pattern of behavior, bumping along the rutted road. "Rough, ain't it?" said Corcoran. "Better have another to smooth out the bumps."

The Ford jounced on. Corcoran began to yawn. "Can you drive?" he asked his passenger.

"Wel-ll," was the cautious response, "guess so."

"Then," said Corcoran, "you take over and I'll sleep awhile." And sliding over, he dozed.

Suddenly he was awakened by the Ford's crazy careening from dune to dune, and with alarm he saw that the headlights had gone out.

"Stop!" he cried, "The lights are out—!"

"Oh," replied his friend of the road, kicking aside the empty jug and serenely steering onward, "that don't make no difference to me, son. I been *blind* for forty years!"

SHOSHONE JOHNNY

On an ancient bony horse with a gargoyle face, Shoshone Johnny, the old Panamint Indian, rode in daily and waited for lunch, although he ate so little it seemed hardly worth his while. "Old man no need much," he explained. "Save 'em for young man, so he get strong." To Johnny, the world's harvest was just like his own crop of mesquite beans and pine-nuts, barely enough for the young and strong—none to spare for the old and weak.

Times had always been lean for Johnny. As a little boy, he had learned to trap wood-rats and mice and set deadfalls for coyotes—"pretty tough, but you eat 'em if you get hungry." Mountain sheep were difficult to stalk on the craggy peaks at close enough range for the three-foot juniper bow and greasewood-tipped arrow of the Panamints. So, in years of drouth when grass-seed failed, and in the off years of the pine-nut harvest, the Indians were in sorry straits. Then they would "boil 'em brush, plants, most anything, three times, throw away water, eat 'em—they no hurt you then."

BURRO BILL AND ME

Although Johnny now had a rifle, he was too old to hunt. He was the poorest of the Indians, mainly because on his domain (his by virtue of ancestral occupation) there was left no tillable patch of land at any water hole. White men had taken up water claims for their mines and his ancestral camp at Furnace Creek was now the property of the great Pacific Borax Company. To the north, John Hunter had a garden at the head of Cottonwood Canyon; to the south lay Hungry Bill's Ranch—both inaccessible save by rough pack-trail. Johnny's water holes had been too accessible—too close to valuable ore deposits.

"Doesn't the government help you, Johnny?" we asked.

"No—no help. Gov-munt help you, they say you live on reservation. No like that. They make kids go school at Riverside. Kids no used to live in house—they live in house—they get TB—they die. No like kids to leave home."

Johnny's kids were his four grandchildren, the offspring of his daughter, Mollie. They were a family of United Nations. One was a bright, half-Swedish boy, one an impish half-Jewish child with straight Indian hair that had an irresistible impulse to curl up on the ends. There was also a half-Irish lad, and a baby whose nationality we did not discover. Mollie's sister Annie, a mere child herself, was now carrying her first child. This was the tragedy of their poverty; these two girls, born to a bitterly Spartan existence, longed for a bit of bright ribbon, a lipstick, or a pack of cigarettes. The only way they knew to obtain them was by a visit to the camps of the white man. Inevitably another mouth to feed, another trip to the white man as the baby's needs grew for canned milk, warm clothing and occasional oranges. Always the first question was, "How much you pay?" for these pitiful dollars, condescendingly given, meant a touch of brightness in the girls' drab raiment, a tiny luxury for their children.

No one, least of all old Johnny, blamed the girls. As mothers, they could set an example for many a white woman I had known, with husband, home and income. In their bare brush wickiup, devoid of every comfort, reigned family peace and utter devotion. Seldom were the children scolded, never were they spanked, yet their respect was invariable, their obedience instant. From the first year of life, spent strapped to a woven willow board, to the tenth year, the child was his mother's. In the tenth year, a boy became a "vaquero" and thereafter rode with the men, assuming the duties of the hunt instead of his former camp tasks.

One day Johnny came into camp and sank dejectedly in the sand. "Me sick," he said sadly. "Me eat too much fresh sheep— think mebbe so me die. Get 'em brush—boil 'em—make 'em soup—take everything out" (gesture of removing the stomach through the esophagus). "Me pretty good, now." Silence awhile. Then, "Me lose 'em weight—pat (fat) all go away" (sweeping the fat slowly from his body with a long downward gesture) "but" (brightening) "he no get away now. Me ketch 'em. See?" And Johnny rolled up his pants leg to display the trap he had set to catch his own fat on its downward course—both legs tightly encased in neat canvas spirals from knee to toe!

One day as we sat hunched over a little campfire, Bill poked idly at a mesquite bug, standing on its head as mesquite bugs do. Johnny reached for Bill's hand.

"Don't hurt," he implored. "He good bug."

"What's he good for, Johnny?"

Settling himself comfortably on the sand, Johnny began: "Long time ago, coyote he see mesquite bug. He go around the mesquite bush, around the greasewood, all day he go around and around, follow mesquite bug, so pretty soon he can catch him. Mesquite bug, he see coyote, so he go around the bushes, and he keep always just a little ahead of coyote. Finally, coyote get real close, he just going to jump on mesquite bug and mesquite bug he see he no get away. So he stick his head down in sand, just like that one, and he say, 'Sh sh sh! Sh, coyote, don't you bother me—somebody talk down here and I listen.' Coyote he go away and ever since then nobody bother mesquite bug when he listen."

From Shoshone Johnny, we learned whence came the springs of the desert and the streams of the forest country so far to the north across the white-capped Sierras.

"Like this," reflected Johnny, squatting on his heels and tracing a stick through the sand. "Long time ago, my people, my old people's people, all dying—no water—no water anywhere. My old people call a big pow-wow, they ask the fastest runners how soon they can go with water baskets to the Big Water at the edge of Setting Sun, and bring back water for the people. Runners all shake heads—no, they no can do. Everybody die before they get back.

"Then they ask the Devil—soon can he go? He say, yes, he go—so the Devil he take big water basket, tie around his head, he go very fast to Big Water at edge of Setting Sun. He fill basket, put 'em on head, and he take big steps from top of one mountain to top of next mountain.

"When he get to Argus Range, he sit down to rest, and he

SHOSHONE JOHNNY

loaded so heavy he leave big print of where he sat, and print of elbow—still there—I see 'em lotsa times. When he get up, he not walk so steady—he tired now—so sometimes he spill a little drop. Everytime a drop fall, a spring come up through the ground, and ever since that time springs are here in this country.

"When the Devil get away up to other Indians called Monos, he dump his water basket, and water run into all dry lakes and streams, and ever since then they no stop running—always water for all the people."

Johnny's voice trailed into a silence broken only by the bubbling of Wild Rose Spring in its cement-walled prison. Johnny's gnarled old hand went out in a slight gesture toward the sound. "See," he repeated quietly, "always water now for all the people."

"We bought new tires in Beatty, Nevada. Thirty-five miles later this is all we had left. Now in Death Valley Museum." 1931.

Neighbor Shorty Borden was also a partner with Bill on lead-silver claims in Hanapaugh Canyon.

Bill trapped a black and white burro at a water hole in Wild Rose Canyon. They tied him to old Annie and in three days Balboa was trained to lead.

"FOUR FEET OF CALICO"

MICE AND MEN

Gradually our pattern of life conformed to that of the country, and when at last our old alarm clock gave up the ghost and even George could fix it no more, we were surprised to find that we did not miss it. For the first time we realized how bound we had been to the inexorable hands of time on the face of clock after clock. Now, we rose with the birds, ate when we were hungry, went inside only when it grew dark. At night, we read by the light of a coal oil lamp the Saturday Evening Post, the Literary Digest or Colliers—they were cheap and good reading. Rarely did we see a newspaper. Our car radio was the first radio in that country. Yet we seldom listened to it. When soft music came floating in from another world—a world of women, bathed, perfumed, waved, and clothed in soft clinging dresses, it made me slightly uncomfortable when I looked at my harsh hands, my heavy hobnailed boots and rough dried chambray shirts and jeans. I turned off the music and looked at the moon etching a sparse line of vegetation on our canyon rim, or I went inside to watch the mice.

When we had first moved into our shack, there had been a

mouse. Now, by the light of the oil lamp set upon the floor, we could count thirty-six, scampering for the pine nuts that we scattered for them. We liked their bright intelligent little faces peering down from the rafters and peeking from behind the stove, until one night they found their way into the bacon sack.

On the desert, a man's bacon sack is his life's blood, and woe betide anything that gets into it. Ours hung from the center rafter by a heavy wire. How did the mice get down that length of wire into the sack and out again? We sat up late one night to find out, and at last after all the others had gone away for the night, there came slipping along the rafter one little gray shadow. Creeping stealthily to the wire that fastened around the rafter, he grasped it in both little pink paws, took a turn around it with his tail, and hurriedly snubbed himself down, hand over hand, into the open canvas sack. After he had gorged himself, and fouled up the rest, he went out just as he had come in, hand over hand like a monkey on a rope. Bill tried running the wire through a tin can lid, halfway down its length, but after one or two baconless nights the little imp had that figured.

Shinnying down the wire, he came to the tin barrier and paused, lost in contemplation. Then inspiration struck, and using the tin lid as a springboard, he dived head first into the sack.

"We've got him fouled this time," triumphed Bill.

In a few moments a very distended little mouse came climbing monkey-wise up the wire. Again he met the obstacle and again he paused to ponder. Solution was swifter than before. Quick as a flash, he took a tight twist on the wire with his tail, threw himself outward and backward to clear the edge of the tin rim, reached up and grasped it in both little pink paws. Then he hastily chinned himself onto its slippery surface, seized the wire and merrily resumed his upward way.

I rose up in wrath then, and declared war on mice. Around the studding on the kitchen wall, I nailed coffee cans with about two inches of water in the bottom. In each can I suspended a small piece of cheese on a thread of fine spool cotton. The first night fourteen hapless mice leaped in for the cheese and floundered against the slippery sides of the cans until they drowned. I closed my ears to their splashing death struggle but I could not sleep.

The next night we caught ten. And then, no more. Again we sat up. This time it was far into the night when a solitary little bright-eyes came tripping along the studding and perched himself on the edge of a two-pound can. He peered down at the cheese. He seemed puzzled. He cupped his chin in both tiny paws and pondered. Suddenly the Big Idea struck and little bright-eyes jumped into action. He grasped the almost invisible thread in both paws and, hand over hand, bailed up the cheese like bailing a bucket from a well—ate the tidbit, tossed aside the thread, and ran to the next can.

In despair I went to Mac. He looked reproachful.

"You killed all them mice?" he asked, "Seems like it'd been better to put your bacon in a tin can at night," he admonished mildly.

That was the creed of the desert men—live and let live, man and beast. Once when we walked up to Shorty Harris' shack, we found him making pancakes from his last bit of flour, to feed an old stray burro.

"He's old and his teeth are gone—like me," he explained with a twinkle in his bright blue eyes. "Too many years scratchin' a livin' from the desert, I reckon."

Edna in the Cottonwood Range, Death Valley. 1931.

SCRATCHIN' A LIVIN'

"Scratchin's the word for it," chuckled old Dan Driscoll. "We old fellows have scratched out fortunes from these hills——but we put 'em right back in again. That's a prospector for you— whatever he takes out of one hole, he puts back in another. Always scratchin'."

It was a precarious life, this digging a living from the earth. There were weeks, months, of combing the hills for a likely-looking outcropping. Then the laborious tunneling into the earth, and if the hole yielded up a little free gold in crumbly red hematite ore, there was the slow hand-crushing and panning, and at last the precious dust was mixed with quicksilver into an amalgam which must then be run through a homemade retort, and the resulting button was ready for the Mint.

Sometimes it was better to find a grubstaker to feed a man while he searched and dug, in exchange for half the findings, but grubstakers were no longer easy to come by. The day of the gold gambler had passed.

BURRO BILL AND ME

Nowadays when a man sold a claim to a regular mining company, he got paid only for the ore he had on the dump and that blocked out by means of tunnels that exposed the pay-dirt. The only chance the buyer took was the chance of finding more than he had paid for. It had taken Pete Augeberry thirty years, single-handed, to block out the hundred and twenty thousand he had refused for his mine. That is pay at the rate of four thousand a year, but thirty years is a long time to wait for pay day.

Prospecting was a slim living—but fun. If a prospector wanted to hole up and live on beans instead of working, who was there to care? He could spend long lazy days, squatting in the sand, chewing reflectively on a twig, talking of the great days that were past, or he could pick up a neighbor with nothing to do and go off to one of the dead mining camps in search of something that he could use, such as picks, shovels, dishes, wooden powder boxes for seats, or even the heavy machine belting that Mac used for tidy kitchen linoleum. It was always more fun to salvage old stuff than to buy new.

Shorty Borden, at sixty-five, was still a tireless searcher for gold. He picked up some stray burros one day, threw on his packs, and came for Bill to accompany him. At the end of a week Bill was back full of tales of Shorty's efficiency. He reported that while he was watering and hobbling the burros, Shorty would have the packs neatly arranged into a little kitchen, a hole dug with coals in it for his Dutch oven, and by the time Bill returned there would be bacon and fried potatoes and Shorty's matchless sourdough biscuits browned to a T and piping hot. Shorty knew from instinct just when to lift the lid from his Dutch oven so that always without a single peek he brought forth his biscuits at precisely the moment of perfection, even though the baking time might vary with the kind of fuel. Shorty had cooked ninety percent of his life's meals in the open. I wondered if we could ever learn, even with this past master as our tutor.

For, together, Bill and Shorty had taken up lead-silver claims in Hanapaugh Canyon on the Death Valley slope which officially inaugurated us, too, as "desert rats" and prospectors.

Eventually, Mac "struck a pocket" and sent off a button to the Mint in San Francisco. When his check came, Mac headed his old Overland to Trona for supplies. It was seldom that anyone, save George, went to the "inside" for supplies oftener than once a month, so a trip to town was a great event and the signal for everyone from two to twenty miles away to converge on the returning traveler in time for dinner. Always he brought fresh vegetables for one meal, wrapped in wet gunny sacks, and a piece of fresh meat, unwrapped and exposed to the hot desert wind drying a coating to seal it against spoilage on the way. Until someone else went in, there was only monotonous canned and dried foods.

When Mac had his new supplies all nicely arranged on his shelves, he came down and invited us up to see his grub. This was part of the ceremony of getting in supplies. Mac had his cans of milk, corned beef, tomatoes and peaches all pulled to the front of the shelves to make a good showing, and in a prominent place, smack in the middle, stood another canned ham, which was regarded with due reverence. We counted the cans of milk and tomatoes, carefully noted the brands and read the labels admiringly, and told Mac that when we got our next supply we would return the compliment and invite him over to see ours.

Mac agreed rather guardedly that he would be waiting for this special occasion, but we knew that he suspected the low state of our finances and was expecting to see us bound any day for Los Angeles or San Francisco to go back to work. We had seen him secretly counting the cans upon our shelves, noting the absence of luxuries, silently estimating how long we could hold out.

Every time we went away for the day, Mac came down and carried home our pick, shovel, axe and other tools. When we came back, Bill always went up to Mac's and asked, "Mac, may I borrow some tools for a few days?" Mac would nod guilelessly toward his tool shed, whereupon Bill would go out and retrieve his belongings with a cheerful, "Thanks, Mac." We were fully aware that Mac was not dishonest, but never knowing when we might take off for good, he was determined to be first to put in a claim for our abandoned equipment.

A BURRO AND
A BUSINESS

Bill wanted a burro of his own, and one day he asked Shoshone Johnny if he would sell us one of his. The next day Johnny came to our camp on his old rack-of-bones horse, leading the neatest, trimmest little mouse-gray burro we had ever seen. "How come you sell him, Johnny?" queried Bill a trifle suspiciously. "He no good?"

"Him good," replied Johnny impassively, "but he no stay with other burros. All time he like to be alone. Good for you—he stay with you."

"What's his name?" asked Bill.

"Burro," responded Johnny.

"What's he eat?" persisted Bill, for as yet we knew nothing about these little beasts of burden.

"Apples," replied Johnny, without a change of expression.

BURRO BILL AND ME

"Apples!" cried Bill, "No apples in Wild Rose—no apples in Death Valley, Johnny!"

"Apples," maintained Johnny stoutly. So our burro became "Apple-Jack," which was soon shortened to Jack as his apple-less diet continued.

With Jack to carry our water, grub and bed-roll, Bill and I made trips into every old mining camp on both slopes of the Panamints, sleeping under the stars, caring not where night overtook us, since we had with us all that we needed. From these trips we brought back beautiful specimens of copper, gold, silver, lead, feldspar and many other minerals formerly mined in these wrinkled hills. Also, there were treasures that we could not resist—old whiskey bottles, hand pressed hip-flasks, and pickle bottles colored purple by the sun, kerosene shaft lanterns, rusted picks, shovels and gold-pans, queer little fish-hook cactus plants, and once a lovely specimen of what seemed to be fossil seaweed. Soon our shack at Wild Rose was bulging with our junk, as Mac called it. Yet even he caught the collecting fever and came in one day with a pair of strange handmade skis that he had found on the slopes of Telescope Peak.

Bill's mind never functioned well on a full stomach, but now that we were down to the last bean, he lay awake nights figuring ways to buy food, or better yet, ways to get along without having to buy any. I preferred the kinds of food acquired by cash transaction, so I encouraged Bill's latest scheme.

"We are going into business," he announced. "We don't need a dime to do it. People will tell you what they want—and tourists are always wanting souvenirs. We have all these relics, purple bottles and ore specimens—let's move down into Death Valley, take up squatter's rights, build a trading post and sell this stuff."

"Build with what?" I queried.

"Lumber and tin from the abandoned mining camps," retorted Bill complacently.

For days we scurried around the hills salvaging old lumber, tin and other materials with which to build our trading post. Two miners gathered it up in their old truck and transported it to a lonely dune that Bill had selected at Salt Creek Crossing on the floor of Death Valley.

At sunset they dumped me there and Bill went back up the mountain to bring down our Ford—the little Model-T that had replaced our snappy Model-A Ford coupe as times grew lean. They rumbled off and there I sat, amid piles of tin and weathered lumber, bottles, rusted relics and ore—a squatter on the public domain.

Around the bend in the road clattered a lone car. Its occupants turned and stared to see a woman sitting alone miles from anywhere, without home, shelter, or even a car—but they did not stop. The stars came out and from the shadowy gray dunes above, to the distant alkali wastes below, they were the only light in all the world. Silence beat steadily upon my eardrums, insistent, rhythmic, like a giant pulsebeat. Sometimes it sounded like bells but when I rose to listen carefully, there was only the pulsing stillness.

I made my bed upon the sand and slept.

At daylight, Bill was back and after breakfast he went to Beatty, Nevada, on the opposite edge of the Valley, for nails. At dark he returned, but not alone. He unloaded a big lank bindlestiff whom he introduced only as Slim. Slim had been heading the other way, but in the agreeable manner of bindlestiffs with no particular destination, he had volunteered to turn around and come back with Bill. He was wonderful at building and in a few days there stood our house, barely large enough for a bed.

"Is that all of it?" I asked. "No other room?"

"Nope," responded Slim cheerily, "you don't need one. We'll fold the bed up and the table down—you don't eat and sleep at the same time, do you?"

There was no answer to that and I subsided.

That was the way Slim took over. He furnished our outdoor kitchen with pots and pans, spoons and cups made from tin cans and hay-wire. With a pair of pliers and a few tin cans Slim could set up housekeeping anywhere. But how he could eat! Once he had made four hundred dollars in the Fallon hay-fields, so he "shacked up" till he'd eaten the whole four hundred bucks, he said. He practically drooled telling us about the daily half dozen scrambled eggs topped off with jam "just lousy with real strawberries"—sort of reproaching us for not doing as well by him.

When the house was done, Bill and Slim went up to the dunes and salvaged a half mile of the old Rhyolite-Skidoo telephone line, dragging it home behind the Ford. Then they made a trip out onto the salt marsh for bundles of reeds which they bound together and laced onto the arbor roof with strands of the heavy wire. Before they were done, a raging sandstorm had whipped in from the north, sending the reeds flying in every direction and coating the brown barn paint we had used to homogenize our building materials, with a thick finish of sand. Bill stood off and studied the result, and then picking up a handful of sand he went all around the building, covering up the spots that Nature had missed. "It's a perfect job of antiquing," he exclaimed with satisfaction. "This place looks like a real forty-niner now."

After the storm, the boys replaced the reed roof, lacing it down more solidly than before, and under it they displayed our wares.

From the mesquite corner posts hung our best purple bottles, colored by years of exposure to the desert air. Tourists said they had absorbed the ultra-violet rays of the sun, but the U.S. Geological Survey said that the glass contained manganese which had oxidized to a manganic compound, purple even in the laboratory. On a plank table we piled soft gray talc, amethyst crystals, blue copper, pink and white cinnabar, and other jewel-like colors from nearby mines. In front, we made a tiny garden of various cacti brought from the hills, for there were none in the Valley.

At a hitching-post stood little Jack the burro, saddled and apparently ready to take off on a prospecting trip at a moment's notice. The only thing we had to buy was an assortment of Frasher's postcards and we were ready for business. Our cash balance on opening day was exactly nine dollars.

A postcard sent to Bill Price from Dick Taylor, Freedonia, Arizona, teasing Bill about moving to Idyllwild, California. August 3, 1949.

Burro Bill pays his respects to another prospector.

TOURISTS CAN'T SEE

Tourists then numbered about six cars a day and Bill expected to stop them one hundred percent. Our position was ideal. In the bend of the road, the tourist could not fail to see us in plenty of time to stop. Bill made it a point, the moment he heard a car coming, to be out tightening up Jack's cinch. Nine times out of ten, the tourist stopped dead in his tracks and called, "Going somewhere?

"Oh, just out to Beatty for water," Bill would reply easily.

"But that's thirty-five miles," they would protest. "How much water can that little animal carry?"

"Twenty gallons," Bill would answer, and before the befuddled tourist had time to figure that this was barely enough to get a man and burro back to camp, he was out nosing through our collection. We never set a price for, to us, the stuff had no value. Interested collectors set their own prices, often to our astonished delight. One morning, two young fellows woke us to ask, "How much for the old pick, shovel and gold-pan over your door?"

BURRO BILL AND ME

Thinking of the yards of telephone wire that secured them against the fierce desert windstorms, Bill exclaimed, "I wouldn't take them down for ten dollars."

"We'll give you ten dollars apiece and take them down ourselves," they offered, and thrusting thirty dollars into Bill's hand they took a pair of pliers and went to work. As they disappeared down the road Bill went out in the mesquites and selected an identical set which he wired into place.

Actually, our water did not come from Beatty save on the days Bill went out for grub. Every second day he left me in charge, and with Jack, hiked five miles to old Stovepipe Wells for twenty gallons of water. Strong with niter, it was poor drinking, but made the most mellow coffee we had ever tasted. We kept our water in a large clay olla under the arbor, a tin cup hanging near. Tourists often infuriated us by drawing off a full cup, only to drink a spoonful and toss the rest upon the ground. We saved every drop of waste water for our dog and burro and even kept a dish filled for the ants and small crawling creatures. This we had learned from Shorty Harris who always filled containers at every water hole and labeled them, "WATER—KEEP FILLED FOR BIRDS AND ANIMALS, PLEASE."

We resented the occasional tourists who accepted our beans and sourdough as a lark and departed with well-filled cars, not the lighter by a single can of sardines. Slim would start vigorously panning gold whenever he heard a car approaching. He really wanted someone to talk to, but even more he wanted a chocolate bar or a tailor-made cigarette. If tourists didn't fall for the gold-pan in action and stop, Slim would jump to his feet, shake his fist, and scream all the sulphurous words he could muster after the departing car.

Once the manageress of Furnace Creek complained, "I gave the Indians some pies left from dinner and do you know, they just sat down and gulped all those pies at once! Why, I thought they'd last days, for dessert!"

We understood the Indians' viewpoint exactly. A pie in the hand was worth two on the morrow, for heat, flies, and sand all conspired to make soft pies a dish for immediate consumption. Furthermore, the lady had never known hunger; that gnawing hunger for some unobtainable food. With the Indians and solitary prospectors, we knew that hunger, and with them we felt a close kinship, coupled with a mild antagonism for all the well-fed people of the world. We were fast becoming part of this country, part of its people, and their struggle was now our own.

Death Valley Scotty and Gene Ward, Sheriff of Clark County, Nevada, in May 1937.

DESERT WISDOM

Bill spent hours digging in the sands around our shack, where under ten feet of drifted sand lay the last camp of the Jayhawkers. Here they had abandoned their ox wagons in the winter of 1849 and here we found the pitiful remains of their passing—bits of ox-chain, rusted wagon tires, once the lid of a huge Dutch oven. These we sold to museums and private collectors. Under the camps of the forty-niners were the ashes of still older camp sites, from which we recovered arrowheads, bits of pottery and stone blades. Once we found a delicate arrowhead imbedded in the skeleton of a small bird. These things were snapped up by collectors as were the fossils of an ancient sea world, which we found all about us on the hard mosaic mesas.

Gradually, Furnace Creek put us on its roster of interesting spots and sent us all its tourists bound for Death Valley Scotty's imposing desert castle, some sixty miles above. Thus we met all the interesting visitors to the Valley. Lincoln Ellsworth, the famous Arctic explorer, spent hours each day squatting on the sand under our arbor, happily cracking up ore in search of a single fleck of gold—although his reputed wealth ran into millions. There were men from the National Geographic Society, botanists from Washington, geologists from Cal-Tech, rock-hounds, bottle collectors and just plain adventurers. From each we gleaned bits of information about his particular interest, our minds soaking up odds and ends of knowledge for practical use in the future. From botanists we learned what plants were edible; from rock-hounds, the minerals and rocks that collectors buy; from geologists, the story found in fossils and the indications of various minerals. From the old burro prospectors we had already learned how to look for the common minerals, gold, silver, copper and lead; we had picked up a knowledge of burros, their lovableness and their perversity. We knew that any strange food or new water must first be tested on them. If burros refuse it, you'd better do the same. They seemed instinctively to know arsenic water, poison berries and loco weed. From the Indians we had learned the art of making sun-dried jerky, and that a man may travel for days on a pocketful of the dried meat and a few pine-nuts. They had taught us how to live from the land, spending money only for flour, coffee, sugar and grease when times grew hard and money scarce.

The desert, too, had taught us her ways. From bitter experience we learned that water in a metal canteen will go bad in summer, giving forth a terrible dead-rat odor and causing the most violent nausea, but that it can be restored to its former sweetness by pouring from one container to another to aerate it.

We found that men have died on the summer sands, not from Mac's "poison miasma," nor from thirst, but from suffocation. Desert travelers who threw themselves on the ground to rest sometimes never rose again, for on the scorching sands the lower the level, the rarer the air. Pets suffered pitifully while some five feet above, man breathed in comparative comfort.

We had learned to take salt, salt, and more salt, to replace that which poured forth in perspiration to cake rapidly in white crusts on woolen shirts and even in the wrinkles of heavy boots. We discovered that woolen is cooler than cotton, and that many old-timers wore long gray underwear all summer long to insulate themselves against the heat.

Stimulated by the constant absorption of new knowledge, our minds were incessantly humming with ideas. Once we found a "Pin-Money Pickle" bottle of the richest deep purple, and immediately sat down and wrote the Pin-Money Pickle Company about it, offering them first chance to buy. In time came a letter inquiring rather tartly just what possible value could be attached to a pickle bottle of a type discontinued thirty years ago, and in effect, "Don't make us laugh—who ever heard of a bottle turning purple?" Chagrined at what we felt to be utter ignorance and lack of imagination, we made no reply. We had envisioned a full page ad in the Saturday Evening Post of a royal purple bottle found in Death Valley, where even the old burro prospectors had packed Pin-Money Pickles across the desert wastes in the precious space allotted only to the *best* of everything. We gave up writing ads and returned to our digging.

In November and December we had to dig to keep warm. Salt Creek was the coldest place on earth that winter. By day we huddled under the open arbor in Hudson Bay coats and avoided the slippery coating of ice that formed where we threw our wash water. At night, dampness from the salt marsh crept into our bones as we hunched over our little campfire, with a sheet of tin at our backs. There was no heat in the tiny room with the folding furniture. Like the tourists, we had heard of Death Valley's summer temperature of 135 degrees, but no one had warned us of its winter cold. Tourists, mind being triumphant over matter, were thinly clad and determinedly enjoying what they firmly believed was "unusually" cool weather.

But that was only in November and December. January brought bright warm days and fewer windstorms. Winds were the bane of our existence. Looking up the Valley on a clear starlit night, suddenly we would feel that slight stirring which is the first warning of a sandstorm, and there on the dunes would be a great yellow wall of sand ascending high into the air and bearing down upon us with such incredible speed and force that we barely had time to dash inside and bolt the door before it came crashing upon us, shrieking, yowling in terrible mounting crescendo, until the world was filled with its noise and fury. Always these storms continued, unabated, from the north, for three days, paused briefly, then came tearing back from the south, their fury partially spent, for three days more.

On these days it was often impossible to go outside, so that we were forced to eat only cold food and go without washing, since we could get no water save the canteen that we always kept by our bed. We could not even open the door lest it be torn from its hinges to sail across the desert in a hundred pieces.

After seeing Slim imprisoned in his tent during one of these storms, I suggested to Bill that perhaps it was time for him to move on. I protested that after all, Slim had had three months' board for ten days' work. Bill turned a deaf ear so I resigned myself to Slim and his habit of making fudge before breakfast from our scant supply of sugar. I cooked the meals he ordered and I said not a word when he bustled out to meet our customers, setting fantastic prices on our merchandise. I even made a determined effort to be nice to him. This sent Bill into a towering rage. "*You'll* have to get rid of that bum!" he commanded. "I'm going up in the hills and I want him gone by the time I get back!"

Secretly overjoyed, I told Slim that we needed his tent for a sick old man who was coming to live with us—and that's how simple it was.

Weeks later came a card. "I am in Portola. Send me a dollar to Merced. Slim."

By April it was sizzling and all day our little dog panted miserably. Various pests had come and gone—the ants, gnats, pack-rats, and hordes of common flies. Now came sidewinders, those devilish little horned rattlers, curling up in the bushes at waist level, and whirring in the moonlight. Our burro, Jack, doubtless kept his own calendar by the coming of all these things, for on April tenth he took to the hills. On April eleventh came the worst pest of all—clouds of huge black horseflies, buzzing like aeroplanes in flight, jabbing furiously, each jab drawing blood. They swarmed our water cans and the damp ground where we threw our wash water. Where was that fellow who wrote, "Death Valley is entirely devoid of life?"

There was nothing to do but shut ourselves into our stifling little room and wait for night, before leaving the Valley.

The Trading Post had served us well. Starting with nine dollars and a pile of useless junk, we had taken in over eight hundred dollars. With our newly acquired knowledge and this stake, we could now work those lead-silver claims we shared with little Shorty Borden.

Bill, his imagination fired by tales of the past, had decided to turn back the pages of history, trade our Ford for a string of burros, and become himself that almost extinct species—a burro prospector.

ONE FORD FOR
SIX BURROS

Since Fords had long since replaced burros, the problem was to find burros, broken to pack, yet young and strong. In Darwin, across the Panamint Valley, the Indians were reported to have just what we wanted.

We found old Charlie Sam, the squaw, only too happy to swap six of her long-idle burros for one good Model-T with Ruxel gear. She had no time for color, romance, nor high adventure. All she wanted was cheap reliable transportation.

More and more I came to see her point. If the Indians would spend more time training their burros, they wouldn't have to spend half their lives chasing them down. An Indian burro does not stop for Whoa, nor any other word. You must slip past him, confront him face to face, and grab him by the hackamore before he has time to recover from his astonishment, and on narrow precipitous trails this is a feat worthy of the speed and agility of a Rocky Mountain goat.

BURRO BILL AND ME

To change course, the Indian system is to run around the burro—while he is trying his darnedest to outrun *you*—stand your ground firmly, wave wildly in the desired direction, while yelling with extreme emphasis, "Alley oop! Ondelay! Pronto! Vamose! Get the hell outa here, you long-eared sonofabitch!" It is the lapse into good old American profanity that finally does the trick.

All this we learned in time, but for the present all that Charlie Sam deemed necessary was the use of a squaw hitch to secure our load, and it did seem an improvement over the improvised knots that Shorty Borden designated as his private invention—the "hilligan" hitch.

Charlie Sam took it for granted that we knew all else that we needed to know—the ways of the sun, the stars, the seasons, and of the animals and plants, and the waters of the earth on which we lived. How could even the stupid hiko (white) man fail to know that which he looked at daily from birth till death?

Darwin's entire population of seventeen old-timers came out to see us off, interested, helpful, even a bit envious, but not at all surprised to see a woman following in their former footsteps. More than one woman had gone out of Darwin on the hurricane deck of a jackass, and the gap of thirty or forty years since was but yesterday to these old men fast nearing the end of life's trail.

We stopped at the general store, took on water and several hundred pounds of groceries. Bill threw our belongings on top, secured the loads and stepped to the head of our procession. I fell in behind the last burro's tail, and we plodded slowly out into the vast unknown future, into a world suddenly grown larger by reason of the slow pace at which we had chosen to view its wonders.

ONE FORD FOR SIX BURROS

Now I began to look about me and to sense that at last we were a part of all this lonely majesty—true, a very tiny part, infinitesimal specks crawling across the ageless sands. Henceforth, we must fight for our existence, fight like the unsheltered animals and reptiles, against relentless sun, shriveling heat, searing sand and savage winds. It was a frightening thought, and all the more so as slowly the knowledge dawned that upon those six plodding little burros depended our very lives; for without them we could not carry food, nor enough water to sustain life for even fifty miles across this barren land. Every jot of knowledge gleaned in the past months was now coming into full use.

In Tuweep Valley heading for the Arizona Strip 1934.

"Through forests of cholla cactus. Arizona Strip."

BURRO PROSPECTORS

Twelve miles out we made camp and took stock of our trade with Charlie Sam. In addition to our first burro, Jack, we had Annie, a cantankerous old jenny with a small nursing colt; young Jenny, as useless a hussy as some of her human counterparts, forever casting an eager eye at wild jacks braying from the hilltops as we passed; but Chub and John were worth a dozen Model-T's, both completely dependable, strong, willing, and good-natured. Chub was short, stubby, as sure-footed as a goat and completely attached to gaunt, long-faced old John, kind and gentle with the wisdom of his many years. Our first burro, Jack, was somewhere in Wild Rose.

Next day we headed toward Hanapaugh Canyon, to spend the summer in helping little Shorty Borden, who single-handed had built a road from our joint claims down to a little well he had dug on the floor of Death Valley. This road was a prodigious piece of labor for so tiny a man, but Shorty's faith in our claims was sufficient to move mountains. Bill had agreed to share the work, and furnish powder, sacks, tools, grub and burro feed, in return for Shorty's know-how, some of which we hoped to absorb.

Passing once more through Wild Rose Canyon to pick up Jack, we saw running on the hills a beautifully patterned black and white jack, young, scrawny and alone. All night he rent the desert air with his raucous braying, and Indians and prospectors alike begged us to catch him and take him along. We knew that sheep men mark every hundred white sheep with a single black one, and count their flocks simply by counting the blacks and multiplying by one hundred. Why not mark our little band of dull-colored animals with this bright gleaming black and white jack, easily seen against the landscape?

Bill trapped him at the water hole and necked him to old Annie with a slip-knot hackamore. Annie, being a crotchety old female, brooked no interference with her desires, so the wild jack, for all his first insane tantrums, had no choice but to knuckle down under her barrage of well-placed kicks at his soft underside. With all the strength in her aged rubbery neck, Annie jerked the slip-knot tight on his nose and jaw, and in three days Balboa (as we called him) was "broke" to respond to the lightest pressure. Thereafter, these two could be seen grazing contentedly about the hills like a pair of Siamese twins.

On the last steep pitch leading down toward Death Valley in the gathering darkness suddenly I pitched headlong and rolled down the hillside, landing squarely on top of a huge cactus plant aptly named the "Devil's Pincushion." Yowling in anguish I waited for Bill to dash to my side. No response for awhile, and then came his impatient voice, "Can't you just lie still till I get the loads off and the burros taken care of?" Bill had already adopted the burro-man's code of "burros first, last and always!"

Some time after our arrival, our burros began to look lank, and since Shorty had taken upon himself the task of feeding them, Bill questioned him about the grain that we had brought in for our own burros and two of Shorty's—a wild-eyed white one called Tule Hole, and toothless, bony old Hanapaugh Jack. Now Shorty loved his burros with all his heart and it developed that instead of dividing the daily measure of grain, he had given it all to Tule Hole and Hanapaugh Jack in a desperate effort to fatten their scrawny frames.

When the second summer ended and winter set in at our claims, Shorty turned up with an enormous old Beacon bathrobe into which he folded old Hanapaugh Jack, front feet in the sleeves, belly cinched with the tasseled cord. Thereafter this grotesque object grazed on the hills, scaring the daylights out of every wild jackass that chanced his way. He became a complete outcast from his own kind, but to Shorty's immense satisfaction he was snug and warm.

Bill and Shorty had dug and sacked tons of likely looking ore before discovering that it ran but twenty-four dollars to the ton, which is darn good ore close to a railroad, but not worth digging seventy-five miles from the single-gauge Tonopah and Tidewater Railroad which ran from Death Valley Junction. So, with the first flake of snow, Shorty left the country and Bill and I descended to Death Valley, choosing a campsite in the heavy mesquite thickets of Bennett's Well, some forty miles south of our abandoned Trading Post at Salt Creek Crossing.

BURRO BILL AND ME

With infinite care, Bill constructed a circular brush wickiup, patterned after those of the old Indians, as a shelter against the terrific winter sandstorms. It was ten feet across, five feet high and roofless, built of bundles of coarse sacetone grass tied together with the same grass and laced onto an arrowweed frame. In the center we built a tiny fire-pit, before which our pack-boxes were placed so that I could sit on one and reach to the others without ever rising into the eye-stinging smoke. That much I had learned from the Indian women who always do their cooking in a squatting position.

When our wickiup was completed, the Indians came from far and near to admire Bill's craftsmanship.

"Just like old Indians," they said. "Better you have tin behind," they warned, "lots warmer."

But Bill stubbornly refused to sacrifice authentic detail to comfort. Forgetting our Salt Creek error, we again opened our door to the north, from which direction came great walls of sand borne by the winds with incredible violence. We soon remedied this by adding a brush fence before the door, and were then able to weather many sandstorms in comparative comfort. That is, about as comfortably as did the burros, who turned their tails to the wind and stuck their heads down into the shelter of their own bodies.

"Comfort" was a word I had long since forgotten.

SACK SHORTS AND
PINK PANTIES

Bill was insistent that I learn to do each of his tasks as well as he did, if possible. This, he assured me, was for my own good. Suppose some day he broke a leg or was snake-bitten and I might have to go on alone for a week's travel? I soon learned that being a burro-man's helpmeet meant not only acquiring all the usual feminine arts, such as baking sour-dough in a hole, making sun-dried jerky, washing clothes on a rock and making shorts out of cement sacks, it also involved learning the ways of the trail.

The first time Bill sent me to picket out the burros on thirty-five foot ropes to graze, I came back triumphant. "I tied a bowline," I announced proudly.

"Fine," said Bill. "Glad you learned."

The next morning Bill went for the burros and returned leading poor old John, his head swollen almost as big as his body from a night of strangulation. I had tied a slip-knot! The next night Bill sent me again and refused to check on my efforts until morning.

"You have to learn to do it right," he announced grimly, "if you kill every last burro in the process." The fact that I *knew* I'd done it right this time didn't prevent me from tossing all night in my blankets, haunted by visions of stiffened burros stretched lifeless at the end of their tethers. I could hardly wait until Bill returned with the living proof that at last I had learned a hitch that bore no resemblance to the hangman's knot.

Eventually I became fairly adept at almost every task but shooting. I disliked guns and could not bring myself to shoot any living thing. It might have been better had I learned since the only rattlesnake I ever killed died of lingering starvation beneath an avalanche of badly-aimed rocks.

Gradually our possessions became fewer and fewer—a camera tripod tossed away, an extra .22 rifle—all the accumulation of stuff we had thought to find useful.

"The more you have, the greater your wants," Bill would grin as he tossed aside another article for which we had no immediate need. Soon we were stripped to the barest of essentials—a few cooking utensils, a little grub, two guns, a tiny tent, the clothes on our backs and one extra set to be worn by either Bill or myself on alternate bath days while our others dried in the sun. Of course there was the indispensable axe, shovel and the bucket that watered the burros and their owners. And there was our medical kit consisting of one anti-venom kit and a dime's worth of iodine. Since he had no razor blades, Bill let his hair and beard grow, a luxuriant fiery red mass which he kept shining clean and carefully combed.

SACK SHORTS AND PINK PANTIES

Bill was exultant. "Free as a bird!" he exclaimed. "All we have to do is toss our worldly goods on the burros and in five minutes we are moving! Who else in the world has so little and still so much?" Always he felt that he was having an experience denied to any but the luckiest of God's creatures.

There was one possession to which I clung, despite Bill's protest—my biscuit bowl. In vain he reminded me that it wasn't really necessary, that Shorty Borden, "the best camp cook in America," mixed his bread in a hole hollowed out of the flour right in the sack. Besides, Diogenes, when he found he could drink from his hands, didn't he get smart and throw away his bowl?

"Yeah," I retorted unmoved, "and Diogenes ended up wearing a barrel! I'll be wearing less than that if you throw away much more!"

And this was literally true, for before we had taken off on our desert wanderings, trunks containing our worldly goods had been shipped to Bill's mother, two thousand miles away, with instructions to open them and use the contents, saving only our books and papers. For all my thirty-odd years on earth, I now owned only three things that belonged to me and me alone—my boots, my toothbrush and my pink panties. And full well I knew that when the latter wore out, the cement-sack shorts would become half mine.

Always in the back of my mind was a creeping little worry. How could we ever go back to civilization with no clothes, no money to buy any, and no transportation but burros? I could see myself riding down San Francisco's Market Street astride a burro, hopping off to present my application for a nursing job, clad in blue jeans and hobnailed boots!

BURRO BILL AND ME

Bill was unruffled. "It's a lot easier to find work than it is to escape it," he proclaimed. "When I need a job, I'll bet I can sit right down by a roadside and rest. First thing you know some busybody will rush up and offer me a job because he can't stand anybody else to be idle when he has so much to do."

As for money, since our ill-fated mining venture, there was still about one hundred and forty dollars held by my brother in Palo Alto and mailed to us at the rate of ten dollars a month. Gone were the luxuries of our Wild Rose days. Our regular thirty-day supply of grub now consisted of fifty pounds of flour, ten pounds of cornmeal, twenty pounds of beans, ten pounds of honey, two pounds of coffee, two pounds of sugar, one gallon of oil, salt, soda and if anything remained of a ten dollar bill it was invested in a few onions, a ten-cent can of cocoa and a small piece of salt pork. Our greatest delicacy was either fried sourdough rolled in sugar or a "cake" of sweetened cocoa-flavored biscuit dough baked in the Dutch oven—and God help me if I ever made one and ate it in Bill's absence—as I once did—just for the sheer pleasure of eating all of it that I could hold.

In the main, our diet was beans and sourdough biscuits which I had learned to make of a feathery lightness, baked to a golden brown in a Dutch oven placed over coals with more coals on the lid. For breakfast we mashed and fried the beans, but for lunch and dinner they were boiled—sometimes seasoned with pine nuts, Indian style. For variety, there was game—ducks on the salt marshes, cottontail rabbits in the mesquites, quail near the water holes.

But also there was, we had heard, a new person abroad—a custodian of the newly-made National Monument. The Indians

70

could not believe that they were no longer to hunt the mountain sheep, the rabbits, the ducks, on this, their own land from the beginning of the world. What would they do for food?

"Well," said Indian Tom, "that man is only one. He no can be everywhere at once. Me, I will eat." We, too, were dependent on game for food, so, like the Indians, Bill continued to hunt, as silently and warily as they. He learned to creep upon a rabbit so stealthily that he rarely missed a shot and, from necessity, developed a marksmanship that could clip a quail's head neatly from its body or catch a duck as it rose in flight.

Bill had tried trapping for coyote pelts to sell, but was sickened when he caught his first coyote and saw the mangled forepaw dangling helpless in the trap. The coyote lay as if dead, and Bill, in his utter ignorance of coyotes, carried it home, imagining he could successfully tame this wild creature. All winter he kept it tied in the mesquite thickets, daily soaking the paw and carrying the indifferent animal into the wickiup to lie by our fire. Why the creature did not suddenly rouse and slash our faces with those terrible clean white fangs will ever remain a mystery. The Indians were aghast at our foolhardiness.

"Nobody ever tame coyote," they said. "They be tame when puppies, but when they grow up, they wild again. You raise 'em— they follow, maybe half-mile behind. Night time they come in camp and rob you—but you no can touch 'em."

"Prospecting in the Mazatals. So you can explain to a Frenchman what a prospector is. This is Mrs. W. M. Price, Payson, Arizona."

ALLEY-OOP FOR THE ARIZONA STRIP!

When Tom, or any Indian, came to our camp, he never failed to stay for lunch, yet, in an Indian camp, we were never asked to eat. One day as we watched Tom's wife making tortillas on a hot iron, Bill asked, "May I taste them, Susie?" Shyly, Susie handed him a tortilla in her floury brown hand and raised pleased dark eyes to his.

"Why is it, Tom," asked Bill curiously, "that Indians never feed a white man?"

Tom looked up from the stick he was whittling. "White man think Indian dirty," he replied briefly and dropped his eyes again.

After this Bill often asked if he might eat with them, and the bond between the two men was fast cemented, so that Tom always said of Bill proudly, "That man is my friend—my *damn good* friend."

73

BURRO BILL AND ME

One day Tom rode into camp leading a scrawny pack horse almost buried under its canvas-covered load.

"Meat!" ejaculated Tom with an expressive wave toward his burden. "Meat for me, meat for you, meat for dog, meat for my cat, meat for coyote, meat for everybody."

He leaped lightly from his saddle and started untying the ropes from his kill. Then I saw protruding from the canvas a horny hoof attached to a furry gray leg. The unmistakable leg of— a burro!

"All time I eat with you," explained Tom. "Now I bring you meat. Tomorrow I bring you beans."

Without a change of expression Bill accepted the forequarter, tenderloin and liver that Tom sought to hand me (the squaw). "Thank you, Tom," he said gravely. "You a *damn good* friend."

The liver was tender and delicious, no different from beef, and so was the loin, although I never ate it without an apologetic glance at our burros, grazing trustingly nearby.

The lazy winter days slipped past as we sat on the clumps of sacetone grass, listening to Indian Tom's stories of his old people. Sometimes I left the two men and rode to Eagle Borax to see Tom's wife. She spoke no English nor did the children, but I would sit a while and help her hem diapers or watch her make tortillas. She giggled and the children clung to my hands—it was companionship of a sort. Tom never talked to me, nor to Susie in our presence, yet she was his mainstay and Tom never made a move without first consulting his wife. It was from her he learned the tales we loved—of the beginning of the world, the coming of the white man, and many others. Susie was the daughter of old Hun-

*Burro Bill and Mrs. Bill bought basic supplies of flour and corn meal
at the Mesquite Grocery to last them for three months.
—M. and F. Wilson Collection, UNLV*

75

"Down this street, we dragged the burros."
Fremont Street, Las Vegas, Nevada. May 1937.

The Prices left Death Valley in January 1934 headed for the Arizona Strip.
The first leg of their journey to Las Vegas, Nevada, took fourteen days.
Fremont Street, early 1930s.
—Logan Collection, UNLV

gry Bill and the granddaughter of that toothless old Indian mentioned in Manly's "Death Valley in '49." Susie spoke with authority.

Between windstorms were the halcyon days of warm sun, balmy air and clear starlit nights that made us want to live in Death Valley forever. But our days there were numbered. Already roads were beginning to push relentless arms up and down the Valley, fingering their way into every secret canyon. Soon the cars would come rolling in great clouds of dust and the brooding stillness would give way to a buzz of activity as the new Park Service set up its smoothly efficient machinery, and forever put a stop to the hunting by which we lived.

Bill had heard of a still more primitive place where the settlers had literally burned their bridges behind them and thumbed their noses at travelers on wheels. To enter this land one must use horses or burros. This was the land in the great bend of the Colorado River, known as the Arizona Strip. This was the land for Bill!

So at the close of January 1934, when the days were again uncomfortably warm and the moon full-bright, we made ready to set forth. It was nightfall when we saddled up Blackie, Chub, John, Jack, Jenny and Balboa, leaving old Annie and her colt to run with the wild burros at Eagle Borax. Mac had taken our little dog. Ishawipe, the coyote, we turned loose, but he refused to go. As we trudged down the white alkali road to the south as far back as we could see in the brilliant moonlight there was still the dark shape of Ishawipe, crouching motionless just where we had left him.

"Alley *Oop! On*delay! Get up, you long-eared bastards!" yelled Bill. The burro bells jangled a response and we were on our way to the most primitive land left in America—the Arizona Strip.

Making venison jerky in Kaibab Forest. 1934.

LOST IN THE
BITTER SEEPS

Fourteen times between Death Valley and Las Vegas, Nevada, the daily mail plane winged overhead, while we toiled below toward the same goal, through hot white alkali sinks, over rugged mountain passes, at an average speed of ten miles each day. On the fourteenth day, just as the mail plane settled down on the plains that give Las Vegas its name, we entered the outskirts of the sprawling adobe village.

The burros had never met bicycles, and at the first sight of men mounted on wheels, they promptly sat down on their haunches and in great sobbing "ee-ee-aws," bawled their terror to the skies. The commotion brought housewives and children on the run, to crowd around with laughter, advice and curious stares at Bill's magnificent curly red beard and long wavy hair, and at me, the wife of his bosom. They pushed the cyclists aside, and only then did the burros consent to arise and resume their tortured progress, cringing and skittering at every crack in strange hard pavements, rolling their eyeballs, and elaborately avoiding imaginary pitfalls on every side.

Roaring with mirth, people fell into line and escorted us on our way, Bill marching as happily as the Pied Piper at the head of the crowd.

Heartily I wished the burros to Hades and myself back in the seclusion of our Death Valley dunes, and catching the amused twinkle in Bill's eyes, for a moment I quite thoroughly wished him with the burros!

Seeing that it would be a superhuman task to drag the burros to the downtown Mesquite Grocery to take on supplies, we camped out of town and had our grub delivered. Since we expected to find no stores for the next three months, we bought one hundred and fifty pounds of flour and ten pounds of corn meal, which would furnish bread for ninety days. This left no room for other food, save honey, dried apricots, a little sugar, tea, oil, and a few cans of corned beef. Bill hoped to find game, as we had done in the supposedly barren Death Valley.

Two days later we stood on the banks of the mighty Colorado, ten miles above unfinished Boulder Dam. Churning with thick red silt, the water seemed more dreadful than any I had ever seen and I asked two young men who were building a boat on the riverbank, "Is this the only water here?"

One gave me a quizzical look. "It's good mountain water from a thousand streams," he said, then seeing my look of distaste at the thick muddy stuff in my cup, he added kindly, "You can settle it in a little while if you'll just add a few drops of canned milk. It seems to precipitate the mud faster." I tried the milk and it worked, although the flavor of red mud lingered on, permeating everything we cooked.

These two boatmen had pioneered travel up the treacherous stream and knew the country ahead as well as any of the younger generation, but they had seen it only from the depths of the river gorges. When we asked if our proposed trip up the Colorado to Pierce's Ferry afoot was feasible, they said that no one to their knowledge had ever attempted this route in recent years although perhaps some of the old-timers might have explored it long ago.

"Why don't you go back and take some other way into the Strip?" the same one asked. "You could go up to Utah and drop down into the Strip. I've heard that there's no way in from Nevada any more—seems a river bridge burned down, and if I know burros, that lets you out."

"You're right," agreed Bill wryly. "It takes half a day to get them across an eighteen-inch irrigation ditch. But I really want to go up the Colorado.

"Just think," he exclaimed eagerly, "in two years all that country will be at the bottom of the new lake behind Boulder Dam. I'd like to see it before it's gone."

"Well," replied Murl Emery briskly, "if that's the way you feel, I say go. You'll make it," he added confidently, scanning our simple equipment, our sturdy boots and hard bodies. "Any two people that just strolled a hundred and sixty miles to start on a hike—" he shook his head in a helpless gesture. "Come on, I'll draw you a map as best I can."

Partly from his knowledge of the river's course, partly from hearsay, Murl Emery made us a crude penciled map, warned us of the great gorges of Iceberg and Boulder Canyons, around which we must detour, and stressed again that we were now heading into a "tough" country with few inhabitants, and water holes few and far apart.

He took the names of our relatives so that word could be sent if we failed to show up at some settlement within three or four months. Then he wrung our hands and wished us well, a trace of envy in his strong young face.

The first day brought us to old Fort Colville, long forgotten head of navigation on the Colorado. From Guaymas, Mexico, steamboats once came to this outpost of the Latter Day Saints, laden with foodstuffs and calicos to be hauled overland to the Mormon outpost of St. George, Utah. Ruins of the old fort still stood beneath a rock-walled "crows nest" overlooking the landing site of the steamboats. Soon this historic spot would lie beneath the impounded waters of Lake Mead.

Bill caught some catfish and we feasted for a day before leaving the river. Our map said, "Colville Wash—detour about fifteen miles." Up the wash we traveled, seeing at times the faint tracks of the old Mormon freight wagons. After several hours Bill felt we should be turning sharply eastward, toward the river, so we took the first wash branching in that direction and followed, until it ended abruptly in a maze of smaller washes spreading finger-wise through yellow sandstone hills. Trying first one and then another, we always ended up before a sheer wall or looking over an impassable precipice.

As last we hit upon one that carried the trail of a band of sheep. So narrow was this trail that once we were forced to un-pack the burros to get them through a slender opening in sandstone walls. Here and there along the way lay a dead sheep, a fuzzy bag of bones.

It seemed to me that we were on the trail of starvation and thirst, but I said nothing. To open my mouth would only mean letting in hot dry air, I thought wearily.

On the first day we had found no water save a briny spring too salty even for the burros. We camped and used it for washing, sparing our canteens of river water.

The second day dragged on, along the trail of dead sheep. By this time, said Bill, we should have covered our detour and been back to the river. Again I stumbled along in hopeless silence, lips tightly closed to save the precious moisture of fast-drying saliva.

Our red river water was nearly gone, barely enough for a drink on the third morning. Dead sheep still marked our way. The burros lagged, dog-tired, thirsty, unable to choke down the scant dry feed. The trail led, by noon, to a seep of bitter dark brown water, hopelessly fouled by the band of sheep ahead. The burros sniffed and turned away. They smelled the sparse, sheep-fouled vegetation and stood—pictures of hopeless hunger. Bill strained sheep-droppings from the water, boiled it and made tea, which we swallowed grimly. Our canteens filled with the same stuff, we went on. The burros sagged under their loads.

I knew their misery—under the eight pounds of tea in my shoulder canteen I was stumbling wearily, lifting each foot as though from a patch of thick glue. I thought with longing of the cool red river water, somewhere pouring through the arid country ahead. Bill looked at me, probing my mind, and said sharply, "Don't think about water—you're just torturing yourself." Deliberately, defiantly, I thought of clear icy water gushing from a huge boulder on the main street of Lone Pine, California. I thought of big white iceboxes filled with dewy bottles of ginger ale and Coca Cola.

I was jerked back to reality by Bill's excited shout, "The river! The river!" Pell-mell, we ran for the banks, falling under the burros' feet to drink beside them from the clay-colored sluggish waters. It was salty! Not too salty to drink—but a bitter disappointment. What had happened to the mighty red river we had left? This stream was thinly spread over a wide quicksand bottom. We were puzzled.

For two days we rested and let the burros browse on the river bank. A cowpuncher rode by and stopped to talk. From him we learned that we had drifted forty-five miles away from our course, and that this was not the Colorado, but a tributary called the Virgin River. Immediately above, it flowed through extensive salt beds from which rough blocks of salt had been quarried for the herds of Nevada and Utah stockmen. This accounted for the salinity of the river and the country through which we had just come.

The cowpuncher was amazed that we had found even one passable wash. "That Bitter Seeps is the worst country on the range," he declared. "Nobody ever goes in there. I went once and thought I'd never find my way out of them yeller hills."

The almost deserted town of St. Thomas lay just eight miles up the Virgin, waiting for the lake waters to wash it from the face of the earth. There was no way across the river, we were told, unless our burros could ford its dangerous quicksand bottom. A horse could do it, but burros, with their tiny hooves, would sink

At the almost deserted town of St. Thomas, this hotel waited to be submerged
by the rising waters walled by Boulder Dam. May 1934.
—Bureau of Reclamation Collection

Ruins of the town of St. Thomas as the waters of Lake Mead rise.
—Elbert Edwards Collection, UNLV

This was the construction stage of Boulder Dam when the Prices started their trip up the Colorado River toward Pierce's Ferry en route to the Arizona Strip.
—Bureau of Reclamation Collection

rapidly into the sucking sand. Our burros, desert-bred, hated water underfoot and would go through the most elaborate antics to cross even a trickle.

There had been a bridge across the river. "But," said the cowherd with a knowing wink, "someone on the other side burned it down 'bout a year ago. God only knows what's going on over there when nobody can't get in and damn few ever come out." Bill's ears pricked up—why, this was the very place we had been headed for ever since we left Death Valley! We had lost our way up the Colorado but unwittingly we had stumbled over the shortest, most direct route to the primitive Arizona Strip. If we could only get those burros across the river!

The few remaining residents of St. Thomas strongly opposed our plan to cross the Virgin. They refused to state their reasons in so many words, but their hints were strong enough. "That Strip ain't healthy," said one. "People live over there that dassent come out. Might be you and your burros'll end up over a cliff. Better stay outa there."

"Shucks," growled Bill, "they're just trying to kid a couple of tenderfeet. Outlaws and rustlers went out years ago."

But his tone lacked conviction.

"Pipe Springs, Arizona. First shade! Taken years after the drought of '34."

At Pipe Springs National Monument, the huge doors once swung open to protect pioneers and their wagons and stock from the Indians. 1934.

LAND OF DROUTH

The real backbone of our expedition was our burro, Old John. Already, with a wisdom born of long experience he had led us safely across precipitous trails, through blinding sandstorms and past arsenic springs. Now, in utter trust, he followed Bill into the quicksand river, hurrying as Bill did, to prevent his feet from sinking into the tugging sands. Together they ferried our camp to the opposite shore, trip by trip, while the other burros gained courage. On the last trip they all went into the water with little fuss, Bill and John pulling while I belabored from the rear with the old familiar, "Alley-oop, ondelay!"

At the end of the day we made camp—just one hundred yards on our way. A rider stopped for supper. "Cripes, them eggs are good!" he exclaimed as he wolfed down his fourth. "Where'd you get 'em?"

"St. Thomas—15 cents a dozen," replied Bill.

"Well," he exulted, "I've got just six bits to my name and I'm headin' right over and get me five dozen eggs. That's the first egg I've et in three months."

"Where you from?" Bill asked.

Then the bitter story poured forth. "I was down around Phoenix with my sheep, and everything dried up—no water, no feed, sheep starvin' to death. The guvmint wants fifty cents a head on public domain, and wool sellin' for fifty cents a pound. I ain't got a cryin' dime and the sheep won't make my salt on fifty-cent wool. But I gotta save them sheep somehow—I've lived with the damn things so long I know every doggone sheep's face better'n I do my own.

"Well, I heard about this Strip bein' all free range, so we just start out, and we've come 400 miles since then and ain't hit no feed yet. The sheep started droppin' off after we'd slipped across the river down near Needles, but the worst place of the whole damn trip—the damnedest place a man ever set foot in—was some little yeller hills in a place they call the Bitter Seeps—"

We interrupted excitedly, "It was you—we followed your sheep through the Bitter Seeps!"

Now we learned that Arizona was in the grip of a terrible drouth; whole herds were doomed, the public grazing domain was leased out to the last acre, and the "free range" on the Strip was grazed to the last spear of grass by 120 thousand head of sheep and thousands of Angora goats brought down from Utah. In all the land there seemed no place for the little man with his rapidly dwindling band of 400 sheep—and lambing time was at hand. We could only wish him luck, our hearts wrung by his misery.

Twenty miles farther on, we stood on the edge of the Grand Wash and looked across at the Grand Cliffs, a towering perpendicular wall extending for 60 miles with only two passes to the plateau above. The Grand Wash was the merging place of thousands of smaller washes and gullies, rapidly eroding the overgrazed land.

On the edge of the wash lay Nay's Ranch, an old Mormon outpost handed down through generations of one family. It, too, was gashed by gullies to the very roots of the orchard trees.

Here lived a kindly young couple and their two small children, as nearly self-sufficient as a family could possibly be. Twice a year, Allen Nay went to civilization for flour, matches and tea, traveling in a rubber-tired wagon made from an old Model-T chassis. They had their own fruit trees, garden, cow, pigs, chickens, sheep, bees, and even salt from the mines we had passed. The young wife washed, carded and spun the wool, made her own clothing, and utilized everything that came her way in true Mormon tradition.

They gave us a cabin to sleep in and brought us some "bottled" fruit, sweetened with honey, and a small sack of jerked beef which we ate ravenously, for it was now weeks since we had eaten any meat save corned beef, a can of which we stretched over three meals.

We had begun to see the meaning of that common range-land expression, "meat-hungry."

To Mrs. Nay, I gave something that had long been in our packs, tenderly wrapped, utterly useless. It was a pair of sheer silk stockings, sent to me in the Death Valley wickiup by my misguided sister in Virginia, with the complacent remark, "Of course you must dress up *sometime.*" Hardly the thing for the rough board seat of Nay's "Mormon" freight wagon, on the sixty-mile dirt road to St. George, Utah, but "I'll put them on when I get there," promised Mrs. Nay happily, touching them lightly with one work-roughened finger.

What the two Nay youngsters lacked in toys and amusements, they more than made up with a lively interest in the world about them. As we left the ranch, they set up a howl and we heard their mother change their mood to one of delight with the soothing promise, "Now, now, be good, and Mother will take you to see a nice old dead cow!"

At night, the awesome stretch of the Grand Wash was lit by brightly blazing fires spaced evenly three miles apart. The herders were warning away hungry coyotes with flaming Joshua trees, the only fuel in that whole parched land.

On our side of the wash there were no herds through miles of giant cholla cactus, and the burros found fair forage until we came to the red hills covered with scrub cedar, that marked the land of the goat-men. Here, as high as a goat could reach by standing on his hind legs, whole areas had been devastated. The goats had moved on. We found them soon after, and the camps of their herders.

The men greeted us with surprise and begged us to stay as long as we liked—adding, "There's plenty of goat meat—but damn poor burro feed."

The goat herders lived in large camp-wagons, built like the old prairie schooners. Inside was a table, bench, stove, and bunk where all the men slept together crosswise of the bed. The food needed no storage space, for they had only biscuits (made with goat grease) and the meat which was wrapped in blankets under the bunk to keep it cool by day after being hung in the chill air at night. This was the diet of the goat herder with mohair at the rock-bottom price of 40 cents a pound.

Some of the herders were mere children. One boy of 13 tended, alone, a herd of 3,000 goats, butchered his meat, cooked his meals, chased his goats over the roughest of hillsides, and had the most remarkable vocabulary of pure profanity we had ever encountered.

It was kidding time and Malta fever had hit the herds. The herders were struggling to get into unfamiliar rubber gloves without tearing them to ribbons, so I taught them the surgeon's trick of filling the glove with water first and letting the fingers displace it as they slipped into place. The men were delighted.

The Angora kids were like little woolly toys, each one hobbled to his own stake, awaiting his mother's return from the range at night. Among those thousands of woolly replicas, each mother found her own with no effort, coming straight as a die to a particular wobbly little "Ma—A." "Goats," the herders told us, "are smarter than sheep. You can fool a sheep with an orphan sewed into her dead lamb's skin, but you can't fool a goat, and these dogies must be raised by hand, or they die in the first few days."

One big lank herder had followed us around for hours, explaining in a serious tone, "Now this is a Dutch oven, and this is jerky," as though we were tourists just arrived via Pullman. At last he cornered us, fixed us with a glittering stare, and whispered dramatically, "Do you know who I am?"

"Why, no," replied Bill, squirming uncomfortably, "who are you?"

"I'm a *fugitive.* I'm a fugitive from *justice,*" he announced with pride. "I creased a guy with my forty-five and they put me in the can. I escaped, hunted up my old hoss, and just rode away. Do you think they'll come after me?"

Bill assured him that he was in a safe place, and he was, for we later learned that Tom had been practically pushed out of the St. George jail by the thrifty city fathers, tired of catering to his enormous appetite.

If Tom was an example, perhaps this country of outlaws was not as ill-omened as we had been led to believe.

*"A one night camp on City Creek in East Verde,
Mazatal Mountain. 1935."*

STRANGERS ARE
SUSPECT

Thus far, the land across the Virgin had presented nothing more sinister than drouth, famine and grinding poverty. In 60 miles, we had seen only two habitations and the temporary camps of the goat herds. Now we were trekking down the eastern edge of the Grand Wash, under the shadows of the Grand Cliffs, forty miles to the next water. The spring sun scorched overhead as we trudged through thick clouds of dust from the burros' heels. Not a sprig of forage was left behind the mighty exodus of 120,000 sheep. Mile after mile, the ground was cut by myriads of tiny sheep trails, crossing and re-crossing in the aimless pattern of grazing herds, until we neared the water. Then the trails became capillaries, leading into veins and larger veins, until at last they merged into three or four wide main arteries streaming toward the heart of that whole range—the water hole at Pakoon Spring.

In that dry brown stretch of broken ridges and gullies, Pakoon gleamed like a bright green jewel. The burros slid over the steep bank of the wash and galloped to water while we followed the longer trail. By the time we arrived, the residents were out to meet us. Here lived another young couple and two small children. They were friendly, cordial and seemed glad to have us camp for a while.

Every morning, the children came shyly to our tent with a jar of warm cow's milk, which vastly improved the jerky gravy that was now our staple three-times-a-day diet. I made it of grease, flour and water and added dried goat meat pounded to a powder between two rocks. It was rib-sticking, but how monotonous! I longed for one meal of bacon, eggs and crisp, crunchy toast and said as much to the rancher's wife, in the course of our womanly confidences.

The next morning, instead of milk, the children brought a note. "Can you come up before you eat?" Bless her heart, the woman had cooked for me the meal I most yearned for—and what matter that the toast was somewhat burned homemade bread and the bacon the ends of a slightly rancid bacon-side? It was heavenly manna to me!

We had told the rancher that we were interested in Indian ruins. He said he knew of none close by, but there was an interesting cave up in the malapai behind the house. "Until eight years ago," he explained, "this place was held by outlaws. Those rock corrals overlooking the spring were their forts. See the gunholes in them? Nobody who came in after them ever went back. What happened, I don't know, but this cave is full of skeletons, I've heard—and *not* Indians, either."

Immediately Bill began laying plans to enter the cave. Armed with a rope, carbide lamp and snake-bite serum, he and the rancher climbed the black malapai slopes while I panted along behind, determined to miss nothing. The cave entrance was merely an opening straight into the earth. Bill stripped to his shorts and wriggled his way downward. For a moment his fingers gripped the rim—then dropped from sight. It seemed a long time before we heard his voice, curiously muffled, "Hold the rope—I'm coming up for air. This dust is terrible."

Once in the air, he described the gruesome cavern. "There are two chambers—the second is the larger. It is full of bones, some all scrambled up and some still distinct skeletons. They can't be very old because one has on a Levi waistband, and one must have worn a silk dress—the buttons are scattered around it."

There was no way to solve this mystery and the rancher seemed glad to let well enough alone.

One day another couple rode in. They had come by horseback over forty miles from their dugout at the head of the wash, they told us, to "eat an egg and get some real coffee." The woman said, "I had just eaten jerky gravy and sourdough and drunk Mormon tea till I cried every time I sat down to another meal of it. I wanted an egg so bad I couldn't stand it—so we just saddled up and rode down to spend a few days with these here chickens." She kept the coffee pot going steadily and all day we could see her slipping toward the kitchen to pour herself another cup. How well I understood!

One morning the rancher said to Bill, "I'm going to the state line to pick up some cattle. Will you folks stay and look after my wife for a few days? We are expecting a new baby sometime soon." We agreed, and he rode off, accompanied by his egg-eating friends. An hour later he returned, alone. Riding directly to our camp, he sat on his horse looking down at Bill. Suddenly, like a gun thrust in the belly, came the astounding question, "How soon can you be leaving?" Hard black eyes stared into Bill's startled blue ones.

"Right now," Bill replied promptly. Terror seized me. What next in this strange land?

Mystified, incredulous, we packed and headed toward Seven Springs.

At Seven Springs we found The Hermit, a tiny gnome of a man. He staggered to the door clad only in a pair of faded blue jeans, to welcome us with a polite flourish, ending on a hiccup.

"'Scuse me," he mumbled, "been trying' out a new batch I just run off. Pretty potent this time, I guess." With another flourish, he led us to his dugout storage room where hung several sacks of jerky. "Help yourself," he urged. "Ain't got no cow jerky. There's sheep, there's horse, there's goat, maybe there's even some burro, but I'd swear to my dyin' day that I ain't got no beef on the place. How could I have when I ain't got no cows?" This with a broad wink. Taking some jerky from a sack, he returned to the shack where he began whittling it into shavings for the gravy I was preparing. "That's new to me," I said. "We pound ours." "So do I when it gets too hard to sliver," he replied. "This is right fresh yet."

Soon I head the Hermit say, "There's a bunch of nice, fat critters over in the next canyon—strayed away from some ranch, I guess, up on top—" and suddenly I enjoyed this fresh jerky that I now knew, without doubt, was not sheep, not horse, not goat, nor yet burro!

As we finished our meal with stewed dried peaches and

98

mulberries picked from the trees around the cabin, the Hermit collapsed. When he was able to talk, he told us that he had been kicked by a horse two days before. Had I taken a good look at his naked torso, I could not have missed the fact that two ribs were protruding awkwardly. Bill and I set to work and got the edges of the ribs together, but we had no adhesive to strap them in place so we bound him in strips of canvas, making a stiff corset which gave him the look of a devilish little mummy.

As the little man recovered from his surgery and his samplings, he gave us a graphic account of Seven Springs in the days of Prohibition.

"Down at Tasi, the next water, some fellers had a still—not a measly little still—one that held a thousand gallons. Them boys was in big business. They had the Colorado guarded at Pierce's Ferry and this was the only way in. I was the lookout, and I kept my horse saddled and tied right behind the big boulder up there back of the house. One day I looked down and there's a car coming down the wash. I grabbed my Winchester and raced for my horse. It was revenuers all right and I laid right behind that rock with my rifle trained on them while they ransacked my whole place. Old Betsy kept as quiet as a mouse and the minute they left, I jumped on her and galloped six miles overland to Tasi and beat them there—they had ten miles to go in deep sand. The boys just grabbed their guns and beat it to the river. They made it, but there wasn't much left of that still when the law got through."

I was startled to realize this was little over a year ago! This— and the cave of bones! Small wonder the men of St. Thomas held this place in such healthy respect.

"Say," Bill asked suddenly, "would you have any idea what

happened at Pakoon?" Then we told him the story—how the rancher had ridden away a friend and in an hour returned a cold-eyed enemy.

The Hermit searched our faces while he seemed to weigh his reply for long minutes. Then he asked abruptly, "Bill, *are* you working for the Cattlemen's Association?"

"Why no," said Bill, bewildered.

"I believe you," said the Hermit, "but there's them that don't. They remember the last Cattlemen's spies that come in here— come in just as you come—only they was posin' as trappers."

While we were digesting this startling bit of information, the Hermit spoke again. "Bill," he tossed it away almost carelessly, "when you get up to the Wildcat Ranch, would you jest as soon fergit that you ever saw the little man at Seven Springs?"

We promised, but a noose seemed tightening around our necks. A cave with human bones behind—and what ahead?

WE MEET THE VILLAIN

Why did the Hermit wish to keep his whereabouts a secret from the Wildcat Ranch? This had me worried and I harped on it.

"Do you suppose," I asked of Bill, "that those 'good' Mormons he told us about live at the Wildcat, and are waiting to turn him over to the law? After all—that was beef jerky. Maybe the 'prohis' are still waiting to catch him on that still he guarded. Maybe—"

Bill was impatient. "It's nothing at all," he declared, "but the same old squabble between the cattlemen and nesters. The Hermit's a nester and of course he eats their beef—didn't he tell you that only a damn fool eats his own meat? But how can they prove it when the meat's all jerked, and an old dry mustang hide flapping on the fence?"

This did not soothe my apprehension. I dreaded the Wildcat Ranch, not for ourselves, but for our impish little friend, the Hermit.

With considerable difficulty, we found the narrow cleft in the Grand Cliffs, through which the trail wound upwards—sometimes over places where the packed burros had to leap like goats—until at last we stood two thousand feet above, on the vast Shivwits plateau.

Here sage and cedar covered the flat cattle lands, but water was even scarcer than in the Grand Wash. The first night brought us to an abandoned ranch house and a well, where we made camp, to the consternation of a mother bird raising a family of five little ones in the swaying inverted bowl of an old kerosene lamp suspended from the cabin ceiling.

Supper over, we spread our bed-roll on the plank floor, directly beneath the nest, and for a little time their sleepy chirpings carried me back to the comfort and security of a Virginia home—a thousand years ago.

Comfort! Security! Words unknown on the Arizona Strip! Would we ever know them again?

At last we saw the Wildcat Ranch, the slow-moving arms of a windmill silhouetted against the sunset sky. It was almost dark when we entered the yard. I hurried to the windmill with the thirsty burros, but Bill held out his hand to stay me.

"Wait," he said uneasily, "there's something queer about this place. Better not water without asking." He looked carefully at the rough board shack, with its gloomy air of temporary occupation. "There's a string of jerky on the back porch—someone must be around—"

"Wot-cher want?" At the surly tones we both jumped. Around the corner of the shack had stepped two rough-looking cowhands, looking us over without much enthusiasm.

"Can we get water and camp for the night?" asked Bill, a little put out at our cool reception.

WE MEET THE VILLAIN

"The boss is away," replied one of the cowhands, grudgingly, "but I reckon you can camp if you camp outside the fence and—if you are movin' at daybreak."

"We'll just water and go on past your ranch to camp," offered Bill, still uneasy.

"You'll play hell gettin' off this ranch tonight. So you jes' as well camp, and leave before sunrise," growled the surly one.

"I don't like this setup," Bill commented to me, with what I thought was a masterpiece of understatement. "The boss must not like visitors much."

Having made camp at a spot well removed from the house, we took no chances in outstaying our welcome, and were up before daybreak, hurrying along the two ruts that served as a road to Mt. Trumbull. A little way out, we slowed to let the burros graze. A shining new pickup roared in on a cloud of dust, and screamed to a stop before us. A man sprang out, dressed as all the men of the cow-country, in faded levis and worn Stetson. But in his face was none of the kindly tolerant humor we had come to expect beneath a Stetson brim.

"How far to Ivanpaugh Spring?" Bill asked quickly.

"Never heard of it," rasped a hard voice. "Lookin' for a place to settle?"

With a quick glance at his menacing expression, Bill hastily disclaimed any such intention.

Cruel stone-gray eyes bored into Bill's face, hard thin lips barely moved to release the warning words, "Be damn sure you don't—*keep movin'!*"

With that, he jumped into his truck and whizzed off at high speed. "Whew!" shivered Bill, "if he's headed for the Wildcat, I'm glad we're gone. Suppose he thought we were trying to nest on one of his water holes?"

"He looks like he'd slit a man's throat for the fun of it," I murmured unhappily.

By noon, we had reached a stagnant pond where a band of goats were kidding. The men were so busy playing midwife to three thousand wailing goats in various stages of labor that they scarcely noticed our arrival. But Bill's curiosity would not wait. "Say, who was the man who passed us at daybreak in a new pickup?"

"Why, that's Jack Weston, the owner of the Wildcat. Did he say anything to you?"

"He told me to keep moving, in no uncertain terms. How much land does he have anyhow?"

"He don't *own* a damned acre, but he claims everything in sight. This is free range, but he squatted, and he's got the old authority right on his hip. Better watch out for Jack, he's mean." His eyes were evasive—almost scared.

After we had left the goat camp some miles behind, lost in the rugged cactus-covered slopes, we heard the sound of galloping hooves, and turned to see one of the herders coming full tilt. He yelled and we waited.

"Say, how'd you like to go to work?" he queried.

"Doing what?" asked Bill.

"Well, I thought you could help with the kidding and your wife could drive the chuck-wagon and cook for the five of us—that's all she'd have to do."

"That's all!" thought I. I could see myself perched on the seat of that mammoth covered wagon—I who had never seen a rein since I was ten years old—guiding four half-wild mustangs up and down hillsides so steep that even an experienced muleskinner would be hard put to keep a wagon upright. I'd seen enough to know that every time the wagon went out, it had to make its own road, and I prayed that Bill wouldn't accept that job for *me*!

"Tell me more," begged Bill. "What do you pay, and how's the food, and what happened to the men I saw this morning?"

"Aw, they quit to go on relief," said the man with disgust. "I'll be honest—I can't pay much. Fifteen dollars a month for the two of you, and that's only if I sell my mohair. If I don't sell, you only get your board, but it's as good as you'll get anywhere—bread, goat meat, maybe a little macaroni to put in your soup now and then—and I give my boys onions, too, There aren't many places that give onions," he tempted.

Bill looked around at the rugged terrain. "How long will a pair of boots last in this country?"

"About a month—that's the limit," admitted the candid goat man.

"Well," said Bill, "our boots are custom-made, and one pair costs more than a month's wages for the two of us. Suppose you don't sell your mohair and our boots are gone—what then?"

"That's right. I hadn't thought of that. Well, no harm askin'," and he galloped back to his wailing charges.

Bill was wistful. "That's an experience we really ought to have. Think what a story a writer could get if he had such an opportunity."

My view was less romantic. "He'd never live to write it," I retorted tartly, "he'd have died of malnutrition! Besides, it's too close to Jack Weston for me."

BURRO BILL AND ME

Just three weeks later, we saw a small-town paper and the mystery of the Wildcat Ranch was solved. Lurid headlines screamed the death of Jack Weston at the hands of a posse, led by the sheriff whom, only hours before, Jack and his woman had handcuffed to a sapling tree and left "for the buzzards to pick."

Somehow the sheriff had escaped and returned with his men to the Wildcat Ranch, where, in a furious gun-battle, the woman was captured and the desperado met his end. On the Wildcat Ranch was discovered an amazing cache of stolen goods, gathered over a period of years, from the towns of three states.

I shuddered to think that the men of St. Thomas had spoken truly when they warned us that "could be you and your burros end up over a cliff and nobody'd ever know what went with you." For had we discovered the secret of the Wildcat as the Hermit undoubtedly had, Jack Weston was a man utterly without mercy.

Years later I picked up a Detective magazine and as I leafed through the pages, suddenly those same cruel eyes above the hard thin lips that years before had snarled at us, "Keep moving," stared out. It was Jack Weston of the Wildcat Ranch.

LAND OF
MILK AND HONEY?

We were now far from the land of "living" waters and hence-forth most of our water would be from the ponds of rainfall saved each year from the late summer rains, far into the next summer. Humans and animals all drank from the same "tank" until, at the year's end, the water was dark, foul, and incredibly thick with myriads of bugs, rotted vegetation and animal dung. The nearest of these tanks was at Mt. Trumbull, a small settlement at the foot of Mt. Trumbull's pine-clad slopes, and the first village since we had left Las Vegas, three months before. Locally, the settlement was known as Bundyville.

In preparation for this, the longest dry stretch we had yet encountered, we made up enough bread to last two days. All night we drank, until our bellies bulged like those of the burros after several trips to the water hole. This trick we had learned in Death Valley—that water taken in great quantities in the cool of the night, distends the tissues and lasts far into the next day. I had an idea that this was the secret of a camel's "second stomach" that I'd heard about in my childhood. Certainly burros know this, and that is why they are said to require very little water.

The first day we pushed the burros steadily on, stopping only once to unload and rest their sweating backs. It seemed cruel, but not so cruel as holding them away from water an extra day. And as Bill said, "God knows it's as hard on us as it is on them."

I wondered.

Up ahead he swung along as always, never missing a step in his light nervous stride, so tireless, almost invincible, that any sympathy seemed completely wasted on him. I trudged along in the rear until my movements seemed automatic, my boots lifting and falling heavily through no will of my own, my dark glasses filled with blinding pools of sweat.

At least we had water to drink, for the burros could pack our water but none for themselves. They were growing weak from the long days without grain, and with such poor forage. There were little hollows in front of their hip bones, and in their gaunt faces their eyes were enormous, resigned, lacklustre, where once they had sparkled with the mischief always generating in their fertile brains.

It was long after the moon came up when Bill called a halt. We had walked thirty miles in one day—ten miles farther than any previous stretch. How did we measure the miles? Simply by counting the actual hours of travel and multiplying by two and a half miles, the average speed of a burro train on level ground.

The second day we tossed off the remaining thirty miles before sunset, in twelve hours of steady travel. By the time we entered Bundyville I was just hitting my stride. I suggested to Bill that we might just as well take a little hike back to Virginia to see my mother. "We could walk in on her in just 100 days!"

As we came into Bundyville's dusty streets, women and children peered from behind the darkened windows of their adobe houses, but one bright young woman in a starched cotton dress leaned on her gate surrounded by five small youngsters, all clamoring to see the donkeys. We stopped and asked, "Can we get water here for ourselves and our burros?"

"That you may," she replied warmly. "The reservoir of gyp (gypsum) water that is used for stock is nearly dry, but there's enough for another day. For yourselves, go right down to my aunt—she has the only well in town, although it's nearly dry, too. The town is moving tomorrow."

"Where to?" asked Bill.

"Any place we can get water," she said promptly. "We have given up all thought of feed for our stock. If they can get water they may survive till the rains come. We will just scatter out at the springs in the mountains, although we hear the cattlemen have them guarded. Some of us can go to relatives in Hurricane. We are related to everyone," she laughed.

"Why do they call this Bundyville?" I asked.

"There are ninety people in this town and we are all Bundys and Iversons! I am an Iverson, but most are Bundys."

Mrs. Iverson offered us a cabin recently vacated by her grandfather. From her aunt we got water; another aunt ran the post office, and still another, the store. Everywhere we went, there were women and children in an amazing ratio, but nowhere did we see any men—or dogs. The "strippers" didn't waste money feeding dogs unless they were working dogs like those of the sheep and goat camps.

At the post office we found no mail. My brother had failed to send our ten dollars and we had been out three months with dried goat meat the only addition to our packs. There was almost nothing left and we had exactly one dollar and forty-one cents. We hastily wrote my brother to send our money to Fredonia, miles ahead. Then we hunted up the little store and with our last money bought flour, salt and pepper. The sweet, faded mother of fifteen children, who ran the store, also gave us a small package wrapped in newspaper.

"I hope you don't mind," she apologized, "but I'm putting in a piece of guv'ment salt pork. That's about all this town's been livin' on lately."

We thanked her and went on our way, happy to find that Uncle Sam was providing for these drouth-stricken people. What was this *relief* we'd heard about now for the second time? As we went out the gate, we caught a glimpse of the woman's husband, hopelessly crippled, sitting in his wheelchair while the tired mother and several of the older children were heading toward the barnyard to prepare the hens, goats and lambs for the morrow's march to water.

As we started down the road, she came running after us and pressed into my hands a two-quart jar of "bottled" peaches. Every year, she explained, she drove the team to Hurricane, forty miles away, and brought back a wagon load of peaches to bottle.

"Anyone on the road like you folks," she said, "always reminds me of our people coming out from Missouri to settle." In

LAND OF MILK AND HONEY?

the land of "milk and honey" that Brigham Young had found for them, I thought, and how did that astute old Saint ever choose such a place as this to plant some of his flock? It just didn't sound like the good business usually credited to the Latter Day Saints.

These, I decided, must be the "good" Mormons the Hermit had promised us. Funny, I had expected "good" Mormons to be like the "good" New Englanders of my early childhood—stern, self-righteous. These were an earthy, humorous people, shrewd in business, clannish—but tolerant, forgiving, letting each man tend to his own salvation. I liked that.

Before we left, to Bill's consternation I blurted out the question that had been troubling me all the time we had been in Bundyville. "Where," I asked, "are all the men?"

"Oh," twinkled Mrs. Iverson brightly, "they are all up at the sawmill." And so they were. We passed it next day—a tiny affair—and there, hard at work, were the men of Bundyville—all four of them.

On the slopes of Mt. Trumbull there was scant feed to be found among the clumps of sage, and higher up, under the pines. But there was water—sweet, cool springs high on the mountainside. At the flowing pipe we found a man, sitting grimly, Winchester across his knees. He rose and asked our business and our destination.

"Help yourself to water and feed your stock whatever you can find," he proffered. "I ain't never turned no traveler away from water. But I don't aim for them blasted polygamous nesters to come up here and use the water that we cattlemen have spent time and money to develop, when they are too damn shiftless to develop their own. This drouth is in its fourth year and they've made no preparation for another summer. We are going to shoot the first one that tries to move in on us, and I ain't a-foolin'."

We didn't tell him that the Bundyville nesters had made the same remark—that they intended to kill any man who tried to keep humans from watering before dumb cattle. It seemed that blood would flow freer than water if the rains were long delayed.

And what of Uncle Sam's benevolent "relief"? "Why that old chin-whiskered so-and-so," blurted Bill, unwrapping his parcel of government meat. "He's putting out salt pork that's green with age, and shiny black bugs tunneling all through it! A starving dog wouldn't touch it!"

Ah, but a hungry homesteader would—and did. This was "Ozark Jim" White who now entered our lives.

A FAMILY BUT NO WIFE

He was cultivating a quilt-sized patch of young rye when he saw us on the sagebrush flat. Leaving his two little mules to nibble at the tender green blades, he shuffled to the gate to meet us—a giant man, all of six feet four, well over 200 weight—with huge blackened paws and immense shovel-like feet encased in broken work shoes. Under a limp and dirty felt hat untidy gray hair straggled to a shaggy soiled beard, roughly chopped as though by an impatient hand. Keen blue eyes beamed a genuine welcome.

"Hello, fellers, come right in and make yourselves to home. Sure is good to see someone 'sides them bloodthirsty cowmen that's roostin' on every fence post nowadays."

He led the way with monumental dignity to a dilapidated one-room shack, bursting at every seam with rubbish, pasteboard boxes, rags, tin cans, the accumulation of years. "Fourteen years ago," he chuckled, "I come out from Oklahoma with a one-eyed

113

mule and a bob-tailed mare hitched to a buckboard, and I been here ever since. Ain't throwed away a thing.

"Call me Jim, Ozark Jim," he added, but we couldn't. To us he was, in his unassailable dignity, "Mr. White." Mr. White lived alone—save for six ragged cats, seven yellow dogs, three little mules, a flock of hens and fifty goats. When Mr. White spoke of his cats, it was with pleasure; when he mentioned his dogs, it was with affection; of his mules he spoke with vast pride, especially of the "Red Devil," a tame little creature that he fondly proclaimed to be a "real outlaw"; but when Mr. White spoke of his goats, it was as a lover speaking of fifty cherished mistresses, all equally dear to his heart. There were Irene, Sally, Mabel, Lurene, Anabel, Mariole, and many whose names I never learned, and many awaiting baptism.

"What is your name?" he asked when he learned that despite my masculine attire, I was really of the feminine gender.

"Humm, Edna. Not bad, but I was hopin' it might be Rosalie or Maybelline. I been waiting to meet some woman with them names so I could name two goats, but," wistfully, "they ain't common names, I reckon."

"Why don't you name them anyhow?" I asked.

Mr. White looked reproachful. "No, I name them all for real women I have met. It's like having a lot of nice women that you know, around all the time."

Seeing the water canteens hanging from a nail, Bill asked, "Where do you get your water?"

"Up on the mountain, just one mile straight up. Takes about all day to climb up and down again, so I only go every three days. When I go, I water the mules and bring back three gallons for myself. The dogs, cats and hens all drink goat milk and the goats go up to water by themselves."

"But how do you get by three days on three gallons?" I puzzled. "We drink that much and you have to cook—and wash—and . . ."

"Ho, ho!" roared Mr. White. "Bless you m'am, I haven't washed for six months! I clean my hands with milk before I do the milking, and I take a bath twice a year. Yes m'am, I'm right clean about myself; twice a year I send out for a complete set of new clothes—underwear, socks, overalls and jumper. Then I take a tub up to the spring, and I take a good bath and change my clothes—weather permitting, that is," he added hastily. "If the weather ain't suitable I just let it all go till the next time."

As he talked he had been making his dinner while I watched, fascinated. Into a bowl he dumped some weevily self-rising flour, and to it he added goat's milk to make huge lumpy biscuits. While these were baking, he drew forth a hunk of the identical tunneled salt pork that we had tossed into the bushes, flecked out a few of its shiny black inhabitants, and calmly sliced and fried it. To the rancid grease he added flour and milk, making a skillet of thick white gravy. Then, since we had declined to eat, he sat down with the skillet before him, and roared to his cats and dogs, "Come and get it!"

In the sight of God and Mr. White, all creatures were created equal. He cut the gravy neatly in half. "Go to it!" he roared and himself fell to it. With an agility born of practice, six cats and seven dogs leaped to the opposite side of the frying pan. "Don't cross the line," warned Mr. White. "You all know your own side of the pan by now."

BURRO BILL AND ME

Bill and I made our camp out in the pines well removed from the pungent goat corral. Every evening the goats came bounding down the mountain to their kids, which Mr. White kept penned for that very purpose—to draw their mothers home at night. After each goat was milked he picked her up and tossed her over the high board fence to her kid. Come morning, he tossed them out again. One day he said to Bill, "Bill, I'm all stove up with double hernia. Could you do my milking tonight?"

After milking the first goat, Bill grasped her by all four legs as he had seen Mr. White do, and raised up—but the goat didn't budge. Bill tried again, and tottered, dropping the goat. Finally, he inched her up over his head, gave a mighty heave, let her fly, and the goat landed neatly on the opposite side of the fence. By the time Bill had milked and tossed all the goats, he was staggering from exhaustion.

"No wonder you have a hernia," he said limply. "Why don't you just cut a swinging door in this board fence and run the goats through it?"

Mr. White shook his head. "Nope, been doin' it this way fourteen years, Bill. Don't see no reason to change now."

When Mr. White learned of our financial predicament he was eager to help. "I ain't got no money and I ain't got no grub. But if you sent to have your money come to Fredonia, you better stay here till you get it. This week you send word out to Tuweep and the stage will take your message to Fredonia. Next week if your money is there, the stage driver will bring it. You can't make Fredonia till the rains come anyhow—there ain't a drop of water for sixty-five miles."

A FAMILY BUT NO WIFE

"But what will we live on," we inquired, "while we are waiting for our mail?"

"Goat's milk," he replied promptly, "the best gol-durned food there is!"

"But how can we pay for it?"

"That's easy," Mr. White replied. "I need some post holes dug and garden planted and some land cleared. You need a goat to take along on that dry stretch, too, so you work out your milk and a goat while you're waiting."

It seemed like a wonderful idea. If we had no water, we could live on goat's milk over the long dry stretch ahead. "We need a dog to herd the goat," mused Bill, so he cleared another acre for one of the yellow dogs. And for a lidless Dutch oven, he dug six post holes. By the time our money arrived, Bill was worn to a shadow from three weeks of hard labor on a stern diet of bread and goat's milk.

One evening we went up to the house to borrow some soap. Mr. White was poring over a Lonely Hearts magazine.

"Tell me," he implored, "you're a woman and you can help me. I'm going to send for me a wife. Now you take the book and pick me out one that you think is right for me."

I took the book and selected a plump widow of 52, with six children. Mr. White shook his shaggy head. "Nope, too old," he said, "but the kids—I would like to have them all ready made. Less trouble that way. I need kids to help me farm."

"But where would you put a wife?" asked Bill, looking pointedly at the odorous tarpaulin-covered bed where Mr. White slept with all the unbroken cats and dogs.

"Oh," replied Mr. White airily, "just build the bed a little wider. I don't aim to put my pets out for no woman."

When Mr. White had made his own selection, a thirty-year-old schoolteacher from Pennsylvania, "unmarried, wants a strong Western Type, willing to take up homestead," I composed the letter (enclosing a picture of Mr. White taken thirty years before) urging her to come out and marry a real he-man of the West.

"Were you ever married?" I asked, now that all barriers were down.

"Why, yes, my boy Roamer lives in Fredonia, but we quarreled years ago and I ain't seen him since."

"Roamer! Roamer indeed! I'll bet some spunky woman put her foot down in Oklahoma and stayed there when the roaming started," I snorted under my breath.

As we turned to leave, Mr. White exclaimed, "Let me see, you wanted some soap. Now I know I've got a cake here somewhere. Ah, here it is!" and he triumphantly produced a crumbling cake of blackish P and G. "Take it and welcome," he urged. "I brought that out from Oklahoma fourteen years ago—just never had no use for it since and I guess I ain't never likely to."

Bill's work was done. The deal was closed. We were now the possessors of an inbred, nameless yellow dog, and Mariole, a wistful white female goat.

REBUTTAL BY A GOAT

Our money had come and the Tuweep stage had shuttled back with our grocery order. Now we had food but we were weak from the long days with so little. The burros were weak too, and our favorite, little Jack, was sick.

Everyone we met opposed our going, warning us that ahead lay sixty-five miles of depleted range and dry tanks. "Wait for the rains," they begged. But this was late June and the drouth was stretching into its fourth year. To wait seemed folly. Our loads were light but they must be even lighter on the lean ridged backs of our starving burros, so we skimped on water and were on our way.

Down the mountain we clattered, food in our packs, bells a-jangle, easy going on the down grade. Mariole trotted along behind, blatting "Ma-a-a" meaning, "Wait for me, you oafs." The yellow dog ranged far and wide, paying no heed to Mariole whom he was supposed to guard with his life, for on her milk depended all—precious Mariole!

When Mariole passed from Mr. White to us, he swore that she

was "pure-bred Toggenberg, the fairest flower of the flock," but I soon decided he was speaking of wall flowers. Mariole was a dingy white goat with pale prominent eyes and a weak trembling chin—no personality at all. Immediately she attached herself to me with that fervor peculiar to frustrated souls, and refused to leave me. Resignedly I accompanied her out to graze, rebuking myself for "playing nursemaid to a damn goat."

The bunches of grama grass were some twenty feet apart. Mariole refused to graze unless I went too. She would nibble at one tuft of grass, then turn and call "Ma-a-a" until I walked with her to the next bunch. I tried to slip off and return to camp, but no sooner would I arrive there than I would hear Mariole's little feet pattering along behind, and again that plaintive blatting "Ma-a-a." Bill was convulsed and totally unsympathetic. After all, she didn't call him "Pa-a-a."

We had come to an almost dry tank, not over fifty feet across, and shrunken to a small thick puddle in the center. Cow manure floated on the surface, but Bill hailed the spot with delight. "We'll camp here awhile," he proclaimed. I tried not to show my nausea but Bill could always sense my qualms and he was disgusted.

"You'll have to get over that squeamishness," he told me. "From now on, if the water's wet, it's good water."

Long dry months had shrunken our wooden pack-boxes till the nails were falling out, and the reinforcements of rawhide were curling off. Bill found an old cow hide, board-stiff, with the hair still on, hanging on the corral fence, and he yelped, "Ah! Now we can cover our kyacks!" He plopped the horrid thing into the pond to soak overnight, and calmly proceeded to dip our drinking water from the opposite side of the small pool. I retched and turned away, but that was our water, our only water—and use it I did. Bill's stomach was of cast iron and his will of strong steel. I had no choice.

Our kyacks repaired, another day of travel brought us to that great gorge of Tuweep, and we looked down at undoubtedly the greatest spectacle we had ever seen. Six thousand feet below, the tumultuous Colorado was caught in all its wild grandeur, but from that distance its turbulence was frozen, motionless, like a river carved in mud. No sound from its waters reached our ears.

Down under the rim on a narrow ledge was the "Devil's Bathtub," a clear cold spring of heavenly clean water. Watering the burros was a nerve-wracking experience, for should one shove another as they frequently did at the water hole, someone would be bounced over the edge to Kingdom Come, and I was afraid it might not be Mariole!

At night we spread our bed on the ground, and over it we laid a heavy tarpaulin to keep out the chill night breeze. It was a beautiful starlit night. Mariole crept up on a rocky ledge close by, and while the burro bells tinkled contentedly, we slept.

Suddenly I awoke. "Pit-a-pat, pit-a-pat"—the sound of hailstones on the canvas tarp. "Bill! Bill! Wake up!" I cried. "It's hailing—it's hailing, the rains have come!"

Bill leaped to his feet. "But the stars are shining!" he cried in bewilderment. "It can't be. Ah, *now* I see! Mariole, you get the hell off of my bed!"—and grabbing a twig, he began furiously to sweep from the canvas cover the small pile of "hailstones" directly behind Mariole's squatting form.

BURRO BILL AND ME

I wept with rage. Mariole, not satisfied to haunt me by day, now wanted to sleep by my side and befoul my bed! *Instead of the cross the albatross, about my neck was hung.* To the Mariner, his albatross—to me, Mariole!

Traveling with Mariole became increasingly torturous. At first, she lagged far in the rear, calling to me piteously. Bill tied her to Chub by her horns, whereupon she promptly sat down and waited to be dragged. Chub was too weak to worry with her so he gave her a vicious kick, and my heart melted. I tried leading her myself. She pulled me back one foot for every two that I progressed. We tied her to Old John. He was the most powerful burro and Mariole had to move, but she preferred to do it lying down. When the hair began to wear off one side, she flipped over and wore it off the other.

Old John was growing wrathful. We determined to give her away at the first ranch we found.

Then to add insult to injury, Mariole did the obvious—the thing we had never considered. Mariole went dry. What else could she do, denied enough water to convert into milk? A more practical couple would have killed her and jerked the meat, but not we! We couldn't eat Mariole—even Bill drew the line at that.

We came to another tank, foul and thick. Brushing aside the floating cow manure, we strained the water through a sugar sack, and from a gallon of water got one quart of minute red bugs, not to mention the disintegrated manure and soft mud. While we were boiling the horrible stuff, a rancher rode in. He asked us to "come up and meet the missus—she ain't seen a woman in a long, long time."

REBUTTAL BY A GOAT

When we reached the cabin the rancher's wife came out. "Can the cattle still drink it, Jim?" she inquired anxiously. "Is it thin enough to swallow?"

"Just today," her husband replied gravely. "Tomorrow we move 500 head of cattle and God knows where to."

It seemed no time to visit but they insisted that we stay for lunch, and we saw that they settled the water in a wooden barrel. "Don't you hate to drink that stuff?" I asked the woman. She looked at me queerly. "It's wet," she said simply. "We boil it."

"Will you take a goat off our hands?" asked Bill.

"Have you got a goat out there?" demanded the rancher. "Holy cow, take the damn thing off my ranch—the cows won't eat a bite if they smell that damned animal. They'll starve to death behind one goat."

At last he consented to put Mariole in a corral and notify Mr. White to come and fetch her home. Mariole's brief adventure was ended.

Months later we heard from Mr. White. "I went down and got Mariole," he wrote, "and paid Jim the five dollars he gave you for her."

Another year passed before we again heard of Mr. White. "He heard from some widder back East and she was comin' out to marry the old geezer," said our informant. "He didn't have a car so he sent another old duck in his Model-T to bring the bride from the railhead at Cedar City, Utah. Well, when she stepped off the train, this old guy likes her looks, so he says he's Jim White and by golly, he married her himself!"

And then, later still, across the miles of rangeland, came word once more of Mr. White. He had died at the hands of an armed cattleman in the bitter feud that existed between cattlemen and nesters like Ozark Jim White. I hope Mariole and Inez and Lurene and all the rest of Mr. White's cherished goats now graze by his side in Elysian fields where bright streams flow eternally through lush bunches of grama grass.

Ruins at Ft. Callville prior to flooding by Lake Mead.
—Ray Cutright Collection, UNLV

PROPOSITION
IN PARADISE

We traveled now in complete silence, each wrapped in his own thoughts, too unutterably weary to open our lips. For two days we had followed along ever-deepening cow trails as they converged on tank after tank—bone dry in the shimmering heat.

Jack, the sick burro, now lay down often and had to be helped to his feet and urged on. The dirty water in our cans had begun to smell like something long dead, and no amount of aerating helped. Even the gluey jerky gravy that I so detested, smelled of it, and our long-suffering stomachs had gone on strike and would have no more. I wanted nothing more than to lie down beside Jack and let somebody else worry about getting *me* to water.

Never since we had left the Bitter Seeps had I felt so helpless. Suddenly the long struggle ahead seemed more than I could bear and, overwhelmed by self-pity, I burst into bitter tears.

At the sound Bill whirled in his tracks and demanded gruffly, "Now what's wrong with *you*?"

125

BURRO BILL AND ME

When he got gruff I knew he was worried, and I couldn't tell him that besides the sick burro, he now had me on his hands. So with a dirty red bandana jerked from my hip pocket, I dabbed at my tears and blubbered, "Nothing's the matter. I just want an *onion!*"

"Well, I'll be damned," Bill muttered wonderingly. "Women cry for the damnedest things."

Even in times of drouth, water was spaced no more than three days apart. On the third day, we found a pond full to overflowing with sweet fresh water from a local downpour. It was as red as the clay gullies through which it had poured, and my rice and biscuits had a rich pink color as though mixed with tomato soup.

The pond was fenced and bore a terse sign on the gate, NO SHEEP OR CATTLE TO BE WATERED HERE. We knew that sign meant business and we dared not open the gate to the lean cattle which wandered outside the fence all day, lowing pathetically. A wobbly-legged colt, orphaned by the drouth, walked unsteadily around and around the fenced tank, making soft eager little noises, but when we tried to catch him he ran.

At night our sleep was broken by a herd of wild mustangs filing slowly past, led by a proud young stallion, black in the moonlight. Suddenly they scented us and hooves thundered in wild confusion as they fled on toward their stamping grounds in the Clay Hole country. We wanted to see the wild horse herds ranging there, but heading toward Clay Hole's alkali water was unthinkable after a solid week of filthy pond water and that one pool of red mud.

The next day a passing sheepherder directed us to Pipe

PROPOSITION IN PARADISE

Springs, the nearest thing to Paradise on the Arizona Strip, and but recently made a National Monument. There, he told us, stood an old Mormon fort built in 1869, where giant trees spread a dense shade and clear cold water gushed straight from the earth at the unbelievable rate of one hundred thousand gallons a day. It sounded too good to be true. I would gladly have crawled twenty miles out of our way for shade and clean water.

Miles away we saw the beckoning shade, but our progress was painfully slow as, again and again, we retraced our steps to find crossings over the deep sharp gullies that gnawed cancerously at the stripped earth. The nearer we came, the more terrible grew the desolation all about, until within a few miles of the ranch we saw that even the roots had been dug from the earth by frantic cattle. Yet only four years before, the herder had said, this land had waved in grass to touch a man's stirrups as he rode herd on ten thousand head of fat cattle—the vast tithing herds of the Mormon church.

Even the sick burro seemed to take heart as he saw the one green spot in all this world of devastation. Truly, to travelers who had known the bitterness of drouth for five long months, it was a beautiful sight. The range lay dying, but the ranch that was its heart, struggled on. In the gardens of phlox and four o'clocks, the bees hummed lazily. On an upper balcony two young women sat nursing their babies, murmuring in low voices. There was no other sound save the bright rush of water cascading from a pipe set directly into the sandstone walls of the house.

Soon the custodian came to meet us, and feeling silly at the incongruity of being treated like any other tourists, we signed the register. He pointed out the huge doors that had once swung to on beleagured men, women and children with their horses and wagons, while Indians stormed the windowless outer walls of the fort.

+++++++++

Although there was no feed there, an Indian reservation adjoined the ranch, and behind its fenced boundaries a little grass still grew. Bill went over and returned with a permit to graze our burros for a few days. The custodian offered us an old adobe house to camp in.

Shelter, feed, shade, and wonderful, wonderful water. Wonderful, wonderful world! From the depths of despair to the heights of happiness all in two days' time! Even a washtub to wash our clothes—what more could a woman ask? So long had I rubbed our clothes clean on rocks, kneeling on one gravel-scratched knee, that I knew the day that I again owned a washtub and rub board would be the happiest of my life. Women are domestic souls, try as they will to the contrary.

A few days after we arrived, the ranch took on an air of excitement. The spring roundup was at hand. From miles around, cattlemen came on horseback, driving their spare mounts before them. All day, punchers drove in the lean cattle and their calves, while other men matched the calves to their mothers' brands and still others laid the hot iron to the calves' rumps. Almost simultaneously their ears were notched with the earmark belonging to that brand, and with another swift stroke of a sharp knife the bull calves were stripped of their glands, to make steers for the beef market the following year. These glands were tossed into a bucket, and after a while I saw the cook leave his washtub-size Dutch ovens simmering on the hot coals of the fire, and come to the corral. He picked up the bucket and set down an empty one. Almost in one voice the men began to shout, "Chow ready! Time for mountain oysters!"

"Not yet," grinned the cook. "Give me time to fry 'em, will you?" Bucket in hand, back to his pots he tripped on his high-heeled boots, spurs a-jingle, ten-gallon hat at a rakish angle.

"Bill," I exclaimed, "he's really going to fry those things!"

Bill shushed me with a look. "Mountain oysters," he whispered. "Keep your shirt on. Maybe they'll invite you to dinner."

I shuddered. Sure enough, in the wild scramble that followed the clang of the iron triangle dinner gong, Bill and I were shoved along and took our places in the chow line. The beans were good. I still do not know the taste of the delicacy of roundup time, "mountain oysters." Bill, who never turned down anything anybody else would eat, reported they were "damn good eating."

One morning Bill went out to look for his burros. Scarcely had he left when a shadow fell across the doorway of our adobe shack and I turned from my biscuit dough to see the roundup boss standing there—a tall, balding man, an old man I thought, in the conceit of my thirty-three years. It did not occur to me that he wished anything but to speak to Bill, so I said, "Bill is over on the reservation. Won't you sit down—on the only chair we have?"

He sat. He took off his hat and twirled it nervously on his knees. He seemed most unhappy. What could I say to put this old man at his ease?

I had no chance, for he spoke first. He said, "What do you do about men like us?"

129

"What about men like you?" I repeated, puzzled.

"Men who are woman-hungry," he blurted miserably, and sat on and on into a dead silence. At last my sense of humor came to my rescue and I responded brightly, "Well, I just don't do anything about them. Why should I?"

"Well," he insisted even more wretchedly, "the boys just s'posed—well, they delegated me—. Well, gol durn it ma'am, how do you people make a living? There's thirty-five men down there—well, dammit, woman, are you goin' to turn down seventy dollars?"

I debated. Should I draw myself up in outraged dignity and point to the door? No, you can't be dignified in tattered Levis and faded chambray shirt with biscuit dough sticking to your fingers. So I kneaded away industriously, and murmured in my sweetest tones, "Well, it was nice of you to think of me, but I just wouldn't be any good in that business —. For one thing, I've had no experience, and then it's just not the kind of thing that I'd be interested in—I'm sorry," I added gently. "And here comes Bill. Will you stay and have some coffee?"

But the roundup boss was gone, stumbling backwards into the bed of four-o'clocks, a fiery glow flaming from his dirty shirt collar clear up to the bald spot on top of his head. He even forgot to put on his hat until he was half-way back to the corral, and when a cowhand forgets to wear a hat, his mind is really off the beam.

When I told Bill he snorted, "Why, that old son of a -----." And then he chuckled. "Well, dammit, wife, don't you realize it would have been a worse insult if he hadn't asked you?"

I am still pondering that one.

Chub, jumped Bright Angel Creek,
dumping Edna in the stream.

Bill struggled for two weeks to get a burro onto the suspension bridge over the Colorado River. By blindfolding Old John, he finally succeeded and the other burros followed.

STALKING THE
LARDER

Down from the cool slopes of the Kaibab forest swept shining cars full of alien people out of my past—people from Connecticut, Florida, Virginia, remote now like inhabitants of another planet. Again and again we tried to flag them down to ask for water but, with averted eyes, the drivers stepped on the gas and sped on toward Kanab, not daring to look until they had passed. Then every neck stretched to the rear to see the strange apparitions that were Bill and myself.

Our dry lips had puffed, then split, leaving a thin trickle of blood to cake on our chins in the summer heat. From long days of thirst and weariness, our eyes had settled back in their sockets, giving them the haunted look of dwellers on the Strip. In my hand I carried a single-shot 22 rifle, an innocuous weapon which shot a left-handed curve. Bill, to save his burros every possible pound of weight, carried his 30-30 Savage with a whittled-out pine sight.

BURRO BILL AND ME

So completely had we become absorbed in the life of the Strip that it did not occur to us at once how terrifying we must look to these softly bred Eastern tourists. Having just come from a land where men faced life unafraid, it seemed rather ridiculous to find that elsewhere men were afraid of their fellow beings. Bill was indignant and I was amused.

"What," I inquired, "do you think those tourists from Virginia would have said if they *had* stopped, and I had told them that my sister teaches at William and Mary?"

"Are you of the South Carolina Burro Bills or the Georgia Burro Bills? We don't seem to recall any Virginia Burro Bills," was Bill's succinct report.

At last our signals bore fruit, literally. A truck driver tossed out a paper sack containing five hot hard little peaches which smarted painfully on our bleeding lips.

Soon a green government pickup pulled to a stop, and again we heard the familiar language of the Strip. "Want some water, folks?" No one but a man of the range would speak of water before everything else. We almost fell on his neck. He proved to be an inspector for the Grazing Bureau, and from him we learned that even the Kaibab, long coveted by cattlemen, was now overrun with deer and threatened by a shortage of food.

The cattlemen had warned us that we might be turned back at the forest boundary, since the Kaibab was strictly closed to grazing. But we found the rangers more than willing to help us. They were touched by the plight of our half-starved burros and probably by ours, although they were too polite to suggest as much. Bill asked where we might find a good camp. The ranger speculated a moment, then eyeing the 30-30 rather significantly, replied, "I think you would like either North or South Canyon—good water, pretty good feed, and the deer are as fat as butter. Lonesome though—no one ever goes in there."

A good lonesome place was just what we wanted to do a little hunting, for our supplies were again short. But even though the deer were overrunning the forest we thought the rangers would prefer to be looking the other way while we hunted without license. So away from the highways, far back into the forest we started. Twigs snapping underfoot in the forest stillness sent the yellow dog into paroxysms of terror, and time after time he ran into the woods yelping miserably. Each time we sat down in the shade and let the burros browse on the soft green grass, until he crept out of hiding and rejoined us.

All of our outdoor life together had been spent in the deserts and range-lands, and this forest life was new and beautiful. Soft-eyed does stared but scarcely moved, and once a fawn, surprised in the act of running, froze to attention, one foot lifted, and remained thus motionless for long minutes. Glossy black squirrels with great white plumes ran silently up and down the tall pine trees. These were Kaibab squirrels, we had been told, and just across the Grand Canyon were the Aber squirrels, white with black tails. Never had they been known to cross the great natural barrier of river and gorge.

Once as we sat quietly waiting, a beautiful bushy coyote came into view, playfully boxing at her woolly pup. She scented us and quick as a flash she scuttled her pup into hiding and began to slowly circle around us, sniffing, wondering. We sat perfectly still. She seemed puzzled as to whence came the strange scent. At last she saw us and advanced slowly, bristles up, growling like a dog.

Bill grew nervous and shot the 22 high over her head, at which she turned tail and fled.

"I wouldn't have believed that a coyote would ever rush a man," said Bill, "but that one had me a little worried. She doesn't even look like the scrubby little desert coyotes—more like a wolf. Even these mule-eared deer are built life-size. Some of those old bucks will dress 200 pounds."

Before dropping down into South Canyon we stood for a moment on the crest of the Buckskin Range, 9000 feet above our starting place in Death Valley, and looked back through a break in the trees. There, reaching into the blue distance, lay the Strip with its despairing people, its starving herds and dying ranges. It seemed incredible that step by weary step we had come across the entire width of the Arizona Strip afoot, hundreds of miles from our camp in the Death Valley dunes. Ahead stretched many miles more, for at 9000 feet the summers are short, and by fall we must be out of the cold high plateau country and down in the warm air of the Arizona deserts. We figured we had but six weeks left in the Kaibab, and we intended to spend it in jerking enough venison to see us through the following winter.

For those six weeks we put the busy ground squirrels to shame in our frenzied efforts to lay in our winter's food. Bill wanted to hunt with the 22 since it made little noise in the ringing stillness. Every day he cleaned it and tested it on a small tin can. The first clean shot rang a bull's eye at thirty yards. But once the gun barrel was "leaded" by that first bullet and Bill was out in the forest aiming at a piece of meat, the bullets flew in their old left-handed arc.

One day I was sitting in camp when a wounded deer came

136

hurtling down the trail almost knocking me over. I jumped to my feet, followed his trail of blood, and found him lying in a thicket some distance from our camp. Bill had the guns—and we desperately needed that meat. For a moment, I thought of getting the butcher knife and slipping up to slit his throat. But a deer's windpipe is tough and slippery and I had heard that wounded deer often fight viciously, so I abandoned that idea. Hoping he would lie there while I went for Bill, I started up the trail. But suppose I went to Bill and got in the line of a bullet before he could see me? In an agony of indecision, I spent the next two hours trotting back and forth from the deer to camp, praying for Bill to come and finish off the kill.

When at last he came, I hurried to meet him. "Oh, Bill, there's a buck with a broken leg down in a thicket. Hurry and we'll have some meat."

"Hm, someone else must be hunting," said Bill. "I shot a buck, too, dead on between the eyes, at only fifteen yards. Must have just stunned him for he got away." We found the deer gone but tracked him down, and at dark we had our meat hanging heavily to an aspen tree, ready to be dressed. When Bill skinned it out, there was his own 22 bullet which, aimed between the eyes, had described its old left curve, and wound up in the deer's hind leg. Bill swore with vim and vitriol that never again would he touch that blankety-blank 22. So he cleaned the 30-30 and with only seven shells to his name, began the hunt for our winter jerky.

Bill's method differed from that of the sportsmen. He merely sat quietly, hour after hour, in the aspen groves, waiting for the deer to come to him. The fawns were still young so he wanted no does, but there seemed to be nothing else abroad. Sometimes they circled around and around where he sat, trying to figure out the strange scent of man. They walked with a funny stiff gait, "like an ostrich," I told Bill. Once alarmed, hooves drummed a wild warning as they bounded into the forest.

At last, Bill shot a barren doe, considered by many to be the finest venison obtainable, but to us it was not as good as that first buck, five-pronged and still "in the velvet." Soon we had three more and these four deer Bill had killed with only five bullets. I was proud of his skill, but he only shrugged soberly. "There's no more to killing a deer than shooting an old cow. They just stand and look at you. I could never see any sport to hunting. With me, it's just a case of needing meat."

The venison for jerky was cut into strips and hung on a rack made of green sticks. But making jerky at 9000 feet proved much different from the desert process. Here, almost daily drenching thundershowers made the air humid so that the meat lost no moisture. And yellow jackets and blow-flies were working just as determinedly as we were, in the short weeks of summer. One day we came in to find our meat was not jerky at all, but merely tissue-thin hulls, all the meat hollowed out by swarms of yellow jackets. We made a canvas tent over the rack and built a heavy oak smudge under it, and from then on the meat dried even in the hardest downpours. The smoke in the tent proved too dense for even the hardy yellow jackets.

We kept the hind quarters to eat fresh, and with the fat rich meat strength came flowing back into our bodies. "Ah," Bill would sigh after a full skillet of venison steaks, "there's nothing as satisfying as red meat, sourdough and honey."

I agreed, for on red meat and honey there was no longer any gnawing desire for unobtainable foods. We were as replete as bears ready for winter hibernation.

In 1934, the Prices left the North Rim and traveled with their burros down the Bright Angel Trail.

"When it rained the creek poured under our bed in a raging torrent. See the ice box?" Near Cottonwood, Arizona.

Trapping in the wilderness area of the Mazatals, background for many Zane Grey stories.

THE BURROS REBEL

The burros did not fare so well. They disliked the forest with its soft green feed, in which they found unfamiliar browse and the same strength that a starving man might derive from a diet of fresh lettuce. Desert dwellers feel hemmed in by tall trees. They miss wide vistas and the great inverted bowl of the sky. "I like to see a day's travel ahead and another behind me all the time," Bill would say.

No doubt the burros felt the same, for often they climbed to the highest point and stood gazing off into the blue distance. Nothing in their past had prepared them for the hazards of a deep forest and in time they came to suspect each new tree of harboring some frightful jack-in-the-box coiled for a spring. One day Jack nosed out a nest of yellow jackets which had aroused his curiosity by their steady humming in an old dead log. Paralyzed with fear, he stretched out both forefeet as a shield behind which he hid his tender nose, and stood shaking like the aspen leaves above him. Bill saw at a glance what had happened and rushing to

141

the rescue dragged the burro away by main force, swatting the stinging insects from his twitching hide. Jack was limp with gratitude and for days after he clung to Bill like a lost baby.

One night all the burros came dashing into camp, hopping wildly on their hobbled forefeet, bells a-jangle. Rushing to the fire they huddled over it in a tight little circle and refusing to leave, spent a supperless night smack up against our tent. In the morning light we discovered that Chub bore on his neck five great raking scratches from the claws of a mountain lion.

This encounter left the burros so shaken that Bill was reduced to a quivering jelly of solicitude. He reproached himself for bringing them out of their Death Valley home, across the dreadful barren Strip, into this forest that kept them in a constant state of terror. Now he was sure that the burros would not leave his protective care, so he took off their hobbles and patted them kindly as he choked with tears in his voice, "Poor little sonsabitches! I'm not going to tie you up so you can't defend yourself. Go out and graze."

Like children unexpectedly released from school, they frolicked and romped, delighted to be rid of their restraining straps. Overnight they romped clear out of sight and sound, and for three days we walked in widening circles, trying to pick up their tracks in the forest cover. At last we came upon them, eighteen miles from camp, heading with grim determination back the long trail toward California and home. They stopped short, jerked up their ears, and gazed at us with an air of surprise that plainly said, "Fancy meeting *you* here." Then, catching the relentless glint in Bill's eye, they turned in their tracks and meekly headed back to camp.

THE BURROS REBEL

Fall was settling over the Kaibab. I could tell it by the occasional drifting aspen leaves, by the sharp edges of the brilliant sunshiny days, and by that old familiar nostalgia in my heart. "The melancholy days have come—the saddest of the year" was written for people like me. Maybe it's a feeling peculiar to those raised in harsh New England winters. Bill never approached the winter season with apprehension. He didn't share my worry at the possibility of an early Kaibab snowstorm. But he agreed that our jerky was made and we might as well be on our way.

From the Kaibab side, one approaches the Grand Canyon from its beautiful North Rim. My first glimpse of the cataclysmic view from the rim left me stunned. It was like looking upon the day that God created the Heavens and the Earth. Some are lifted up by its impact; others are made uncomfortable by their own feeling of insignificance. It was such a one we heard speaking overloudly in the vast stillness. "Let's go. Yuh seen it, ain't yuh?"

Going down into the Canyon we met hikers coming up. They were weary and footsore, some limping painfully. Not until now did I realize how tough and hard we had grown. My feet never hurt. Twenty miles was a comfortable day. Bill said anyone can walk that far if he is properly shod, but amateur hikers never were.

Good shoe leather was a fetish with Bill. When we first started on this nomadic life, he had taken me to a small shoemaker where we had been measured for boots that took into account every failing of our posture and bone structure. Only the sturdiest of leather went into these boots, so that the soles were good for a year or more of hard hiking in rough country, and the tops were practically indestructible. Once in three years they

143

were sent back to the shoemaker to be rebuilt. They were our only extravagance but in the long run they were cheap, and without them these years behind the burros could never have been. Watching the limping tourists, I was grateful to the few fine craftsmen left who could make a shoe that fit like the skin beneath.

The tourists looked curiously at us and would have passed without speaking, city fashion, had not Bill yelled at them cheerfully, compelling a reply. This they gave rather shamefacedly, as though unaccustomed to speaking without an introduction. Once or twice we caught a glimpse of two busy fishermen, correctly attired for a canter in Golden Gate Park, fawn breeches and mirrorlike boots. Their steel rods flashed in the sun, their wicker creels were bright and new. The glaring newness repelled me. I had grown used to the soft blue of faded denim and to things worn thin by hard usage. Nowhere on the Strip had there been anything new.

Out of the rocky cliff gushed Roaring Springs to find its way down to the Colorado as Bright Angel Creek. At noon we stopped at a small campground on its banks for lunch. It seemed good to cook in an upright position once more and to eat at a table with no sand in our food. While we were lolling comfortably on the hard benches, the two fishermen dashed up.

"Water!" they gasped. "Where can we get a drink? We've fished all the way down from Roaring Springs and we're nearly choked for a drink." Wordlessly, Bill pointed to the campground faucets filled with water piped directly from the creek. When they had gulped their fill, he asked curiously, "Couldn't you drink from the creek?"

THE BURROS REBEL

"Oh *that,*" responded one, "Why no, we were *fishing* in that!"

Despairingly I thought again of the squirrels of the Grand Canyon—white with black, and black with white, separated irrevocably and forever by an insurmountable barrier. Could I ever recross the gulf I had made—or would I wish to?

The first time we hit one of the many crossings on Bright Angel Creek, I jumped on Chub's back to save taking off my boots. Bill suggested that the burros might also rebel at getting their feet wet, and he thought I should lead them all across from my perch atop Chub. He tied them together and I took the first lead rope in hand and kicked my heels in Chub's ribs. He walked to the bank, put down his nose and examined the water, testing and tasting. He stuck in the tip of one toe and drew it hastily back. I booted him again. With one lightning motion, Chub raised both forefeet straight in the air and jumped, landing squarely on the opposite bank, but minus me! I was left sitting dazedly in midstream, half-crying all the sulphurous screaming oaths I had ever heard in my life, plus a lot of new ones invented on the spur of the moment. It made me feel so good I wondered why I'd never done it before.

On the next eight or ten crossings, I took off my shoes and wincingly waded the pebbly bottom—at which all the burros waded in, brightly unconcerned about getting their own feet wet.

At the bottom of the Canyon there swung a suspension bridge across the tumultuous Colorado. "Now, how the hell," wondered Bill, "are we ever going to get the burros across that? We'll probably wind up by having to go back across the Strip."

"No, no!" I protested. "There must be some other way!"

In a small cabin on the river bank lived the U.S. hydrographer and his wife. They welcomed us with enthusiasm for their days were long and lonely, they said, and they went to the top on muleback but once a month.

"Did any burros ever cross that bridge?" Bill asked.

"Once," replied the man. "A prospector came in and spent a month trying to get them to the other side. He finally rigged up a windlass and cable and windlassed them across with heavy bands around their bellies, like loading cargo on a ship."

"Sounds tough," said Bill. "How about Fred Harvey's pack mules that cross it three times a week? Could I hire them to pull our burros across?"

"Hell, no," replied the hydrographer. "They've lost animals over the Canyon for just such things as that."

With the hydrographer and his wife we spent two happy weeks. She, a pretty little dark-haired woman, was eternally knitting and embroidering on smart handmade clothes, planning for the day when she could return to Phoenix with its familiar life of country clubs, cafes and theaters. She was not happy in her isolation as was her quiet gentle outdoor husband. They had a small daughter in California being seriously trained for professional ballet. While the mother sewed on lovely fairylike costumes for her daughter and herself, I was busily making new underwear for Bill and myself. I had discovered some nice new cement sacks in a pile behind the cabin.

Every daylight hour the hydrographer went to measure the flow of the river. On a steel cable stretched across the water, he swung in a little car, inching it along until he reached midstream. Then he put on a set of earphones connected to a battery, dropped a meter into the water, and listened to the clicking which recorded the rate of the river's flow. At this season the average rate was twelve miles per hour, which makes for a roaring, deafening rush of water. One day he took Bill with him and handed him the earphones. "What do you hear?" he asked.

"The clicking of the meter," answered Bill, "and the rush of water."

"Listen again," urged the hydrographer.

"Why, it's music—faint music," cried Bill. "Where does that come from? Have you a radio somewhere?"

"No, no radio," the man shook his head.

The man slipped the earphones to his own ears again and replied in a quiet voice, "Bill, I don't try to explain some things to myself. When you look daily at a spectacle like the Grand Canyon and this mighty river sweeping toward the sea, you learn to just say 'They *are*' and let it rest at that."

For a long time there was only the deafening rush of waters pouring through the rocky gorge. Between the two men there lay a silence. Words are puny things when a man is with his God.

Homeward from Arizona. 1936.

Near East Verde, Arizona.

TRAVAILS WITH A DONKEY

In the depths of the Grand Canyon, September was a time of stifling summer heat, intensified by the sheer rocky walls on both sides. Yet directly above, on the wooded South Rim we would once more be in a world of approaching winter. It was imperative that we cross that high cold plateau before the snow fell, but it looked as though we had met our Waterloo in the steel suspension bridge, arching gracefully from precipice to precipice across the tumultuous Colorado. After all the hundreds of miles of desert, wasteland and forest behind us, were we now to be stopped by a man-made hazard?

For two weeks Bill had been struggling daily to get even one burro to set foot on the bridge. They had passed through every stage of rebellion known to burrodom and now the moment they found themselves at the end of terra firma and headed out across the waters on the slender ribbon of steel, they automatically

149

dropped to their haunches and prepared to withstand a prolonged siege. Bill had at last resorted to the use of a cruelly compelling slip-knot hackamore with its merciless pressure on nose and jaw. But even for this the burros found a defense, willing themselves into that peculiar cataleptic trance known as "sulling," in which an animal is immune to all sensory perception—as deaf, dumb, blind, and oblivious to pain as any Hindu fakir on his bed of coals. It is the most exasperating thing a burroman has to endure and Bill was maddened to the point of hysteria.

"I'll slit their fool throats and throw them over the cliff," he cried, brandishing his hunting knife perilously close to big Blackie's outstretched neck. "I'll show them—we can walk out without them!"

"Well, you can't show them much after they're dead," I argued reasonably. "I think the burros have their point in this battle. After all, they don't understand engineering. They probably think the bridge will sag and dump them into the river. It's the same thing as asking you to walk a tightrope across Niagara. I bet they think you are trying to make them jump into the river. You're supposed to be a smart human—can't you think of some way to outwit a few dumb burros?"

Bill considered, cooling perceptibly. "Well," he said at last, "I have heard of blindfolding horses when they are frightened. It might work. Remember Old John used to lead any place, just so I went first? Come John, let's try you." And flipping out his red bandana, he folded and tied it over John's wise old rheumy eyes.

"Now," he said, patting John reassuringly, "you and I are going for a little April-Fool hike down the trail and up the trail, and when we hit that bridge again, I hope you don't realize where you are until you are clear out in the middle of it."

Down the trail they marched, Old John uncannily sure-footed, hard on Bill's heels. Soon I saw them bobbing again up the steep winding trail from Bright Angel Creek to the edge of the precipice that joined the bridge. Suddenly John stopped. Bill gave a tug and John teetered uncertainly. Bill gave a smothered oath of excitement and jerked loose the blindfold—at which Old John turned and regarded his three-legged state in obvious astonishment, as though wondering what had become of his missing hind leg. He discovered it hanging helplessly over the edge of the abyss groping for a footing that was not there. Relieved, he drew it hastily back to solid ground and stood shaking in terror.

Again the blindfold was replaced and the downward descent begun. This time, the upgrade trip was accomplished without mishap to the very edge of the bridge. When they hit the steel, Bill kept nonchalantly walking, hoping to deceive John into setting foot on the bridge. Once he found it secure perhaps his fear would pass. John touched one foot to the bridge, and drew back in alarm—the hollow ring had in it something different from the touch of hoof to good earth. He was puzzled. Bill stopped, petting and coaxing, murmuring reassuringly into the burro's long droopy ears. He started again, and this time John followed—hesitantly, fearfully, step by step, until he was at last out in the middle of the narrow span. Only then did Bill remove the blindfold.

John took one frightened look at the river beneath and began to tremble violently, shrinking back from the open mesh of the bridge sides, finally falling to his knees in utter demoralizing ter-

151

ror. From my perch on the edge of the precipice, it seemed an interminable time that Bill coaxed and petted until at last Old John stood erect and tottered gingerly on stiffly braced legs, clear to the opposite side of the river!

The rest of that day was spent in leading John back and forth, back and forth, until at the end of the day, he stepped confidently onto the bridge and walked briskly, unhesitantly, to the opposite shore, where he stood braying eagerly for the other burros to join him.

Seeing that John had miraculously spanned the waters without falling in, the other burros followed, somewhat reluctantly, and after several trial trips we were ready to resume our journey with the morning sun.

+++++++++

From the bottom of the Grand Canyon to the South Rim is only seven miles, but to ascend it in seven hours is a feat for a strong climber. Long before we reached the top my knees were buckling and a terrible lassitude was upon me. I tried riding Chub, whose footing was even surer than my own, but soon his knees also began to waver and his back to sag beneath my weight. The last mile was accomplished in short panting spurts, interspersed by long rests.

Once Bill stepped aside on the narrow trail to let a horseman pass, and made the mistake of taking the outer edge of the trail. The horse wheeled and knocked Bill over the edge of a thousand-foot drop! Quick as a flash, he seized the horse's tail and yelled at the top of his voice, *"GIDDYAP!"* whereupon the terrified horse gave a mighty forward leap and dragged a thoroughly frightened Bill back to safety.

In the little village on the Rim we found our first modern grocery store since leaving Las Vegas. Here were all the beautiful, beautiful cans and jars of food such as we had not tasted for long months. I ran delightedly from shelf to shelf before the awful truth sank in—that all the money we had was seventy-seven cents to see us to Flagstaff, a week's journey away! I made up my mind to buy a loaf of fragrant light bread, that never forgotten delicacy, and a can of baked beans, since in the high altitudes we had not attempted to cook beans. Beans and bread would be cheap and filling, and perhaps there would be enough money to buy a few onions or a dill pickle.

While I was debating this question, whom should I see pushing a well-filled market cart, but the hydrographer's wife from the river. She was on her monthly trip to the Rim for supplies.

"Walk around with me and help me shop," she invited. Then glancing curiously at my bread and beans, "Is that all you want?"

"Yes," I murmured, not wishing to say that I wanted everything on the shelves but had no money.

Soon I was absorbed in her selections and listening to her chatter on about the difficulty of two people eating on a food budget of only sixty dollars a month—to me, who had lived for almost a year on ten dollars a month for two! As she placed the groceries in her basket and stood debating which new ones to choose, I kept up a running fire of comment, half to her and half to myself.

"Oh, salmon!" I exclaimed rapturously. "Did you ever make a salmon souffle? Or do you like it just cold, with a dash of vinegar?

You've bought some chocolate. Why don't you make a red devil's food cake? Don't you just love those little Vienna sausages with French pancakes and plum jam?"

All of a sudden I stopped my chatter in surprise—the woman's sparkling black eyes had grown cold with annoyance. "You must be hungry," she said abruptly and pushed her basket to the opposite side of the store, leaving me standing there, humiliated, flaming-faced, ready to cry. I rushed to the counter, threw down my seventy-seven cents, picked up the change and hurried to the outskirts of the little village where we had made our camp.

"That settles it," I thought. "I don't belong to those people anymore." There flashed to my mind Shoshone Johnny, gnarled and brown, begging a hunk of meat from the big hotel to bring to us—Mr. White sharing his last weevily flour and rancid salt pork; the Bundyville woman bestowing her precious bottled peaches. These were the people to whom my heart reached out. These people were my own.

WORKING FOR BEANS

None but a Walt Whitman could put into words what every follower of the open road feels singing through his heart, as each new day dawns fresh, full of promise, unshadowed by the cares of yesterday. Now that we found ourselves traveling through beautiful open forests, with incredible blue above and rich green beneath, where crystal waters waited our coming, there seemed nothing more to be desired and we wanted all of our friends to share with us in this wonderful adventure. Hunting through the packs, I found some cheap ruled paper and together we composed a dozen letters, urging as many people to plan just such a trip for their next vacation.

"Take a train to Flagstaff," we wrote, "and there take a packsack on your back and follow your nose to the Grand Canyon. Go down into the Canyon, spend two weeks tramping up and down the river as far as you can go, and then out by way of the North Rim to Kanab, Utah, and there catch a bus to wherever you want

155

to go. It is a good easy beginning for a tenderfoot, and once you try such an adventure you will never again want pavements under your feet."

For months afterward we visited every post office along our way, hoping for enthusiastic letters asking for more details, but out of California, Pennsylvania and Virginia came only silence. Perhaps, I told Bill, they were happily unaware of what they were missing in the companionship of six jackasses and one adoring black dog.

For the yellow dog had disappeared, and out of the night had come Slats, a shadowy black figure, limping on tortured bleeding paws. She lay down unobtrusively by our fire, and looked for a long moment into Bill's bearded face. It was plain to see that she was offering her heart. Every time he arose to get more wood for the fire, the dog arose and followed in his every footstep, wincing with pain, but unwilling to lose her self-chosen master.

Bill yearned to keep her, for what man can resist the adoration in a dog's eyes raised to his own? We felt sure that she was some herder's sheep dog, for her manners in camp were exquisite. Although her eyes followed hungrily toward food, she made no move to touch it until it was placed on a tin plate and set directly before her. Even then, she first raised an inquiring gaze and waited for reassurance before falling to. Like all "camp-broke" dogs, she kept her distance from the cooking, and at bedtime took her place quietly at the foot of our bed on a spread saddle blanket, from which point she kept a wary eye on all the small prowlers of the night.

The next day when we had finished packing the burros, Slats

WORKING FOR BEANS

fell into line behind the last burro and limped sedately in our
wake, as naturally as though she had spent her life on the trail. At
every ranch we inquired if a sheep dog had been lost, and at last
we found that our Slats was an odd one of a sheep dog litter, one
of those whose training is never finished due to an unbreakable
habit of running to the head of the sheep band and nipping noses
in the excitement of the work. Word came from her master that
we were welcome to keep her.

And so came into our lives the best dog we ever owned. Now
that there were no sheep to tend, Slats took unto herself various
small tasks, such as searching out the burros each morning and
bringing them back to the trail when they strayed. She became the
self-appointed custodian of our camp, and never again was it
necessary to hang our food in the trees at night to keep it from
foxes and skunks. When we made camp, Slats always made a
preliminary tour of the campsite and a number of times nosed out
a snoozing rattlesnake before I inadvertently sat upon it in the
thick leaf mold. A good dog is the greatest treasure a camper can
ask. Slats made life complete.

Now our funds parceled out by my brother in Palo Alto were
running low. We had been out of Death Valley for nearly a year
and the original $140 had shrunk to $17. Winter was upon us and
I began to worry that, as yet, we had no shelter and no money to
see us through the winter months. Bill said nothing, but as we
approached the next ranch he announced, "They are harvesting
beans. I'm going to work for fifty pounds of beans."

We straggled up to the fence and waited for the one fair-
haired man who was driving a rake. Behind him came a dozen

Mexicans, lazily lifting the raked bean vines into piles. At the end of the row the man stopped and said briefly, "Well?"

"I'd like to work out fifty pounds of beans," said Bill. "Can you use some more help?"

"No," refused the man shortly, "I only use Mexicans." He started to turn away but Bill stopped him again.

"Why," he persisted, "do you use only Mexicans? Can't anyone lift beans as well as a Mexican?"

"Guess so," admitted the farmer, "but you can't mix 'em or there's trouble. I only pay two dollars a day and one American in a bunch of Mexicans would just stir up trouble, and he'd want two-fifty."

"Mister," said Bill earnestly, "when I work, it's all the same to me if I work with Hottentots. And I don't want money—I want beans."

"Well," the farmer calculated shrewdly, "I've got more beans than money. Beans are bringing four cents wholesale. But you couldn't buy 'em for less than five. If you'll work for fifty pounds of beans it's all the same as two-fifty to you, and it's just two dollars to me, at four cents a pound. So we're both satisfied."

"Farmers are the same the world over," grumbled Bill later, "figuring every penny. Wonder if they ever go on a good bust like say, a miner or a lumberjack, and to hell with the cost?"

We made our camp on the hillside and Bill went to work in the field. To the Mexicans he confided that never before had he lifted beans and white teeth flashed in dark understanding faces, as they furtively showed him the proper technique while the farmer's back was turned in his travels down the row. When he turned and faced up the row with the horse-drawn rake, Bill and the Mexicans were busily lifting as though their lives depended on it. Soon Bill noticed that each time the farmer went down the row, the Mexicans all balanced their lifting forks against their bodies and hastily shelled out a few handfuls of beans which they stuffed into their pockets. At intervals, when they went to their old Ford ostensibly to get a drink from the water bags, they emptied their pockets into a gunnysack concealed under the seat.

"Take some," advised one Mexican. "He only pay two dollar. By night, you got ten pounds beans, you got two-fifty, same as other farmers pay. Whatsa difference how you get it, beans or money? Mexicans eat lotsa beans," he added modestly and with infinite satisfaction.

In the meantime I went to the house for water and found that Bill was to eat with the help, so I ate a solitary lunch on my little hilltop. In the afternoon I went for more water and found the farmer's wife frantic with a fretful baby in the midst of her harvest cooking.

"Let me help you," I offered, and although she seemed hesitant, she agreed that I might peel potatoes and wash dishes. As we chatted, I noticed her reserve melting and when she remarked that she had taught school I said, "That makes me feel at home. All my family teach."

"Where?" she asked idly, spooning applesauce into her baby.

"Oh, there's one at Stanford, one at Bucknell, and one at William and Mary," I replied.

At this a slow flush crept over her face and she blurted miserably, "Gee, I guess I was a snob. I was trying to impress you that I taught a little old country school. I just supposed you—My goodness, are you *educated*?"

"No," I laughed, "not I. Only in the school of hard knocks. I've just been exposed to a few people with higher learning."

That night her husband came in and seemed surprised to see his wife and me merrily setting the table for four. He looked at the plates and then at his wife. She rose to the occasion. "Edna and Bill are eating with *us*," she announced firmly.

Although the farmer gracefully accepted our switch from hired hands to household guests, it did not soften him to the extent of giving our burros water from his huge storage tank, freshly filled by a late summer rain. At the end of Bill's ten-hour day, he had to trudge seven miles up the mountain to water the burros at a flowing spring. Not until 2 A.M. did this day end.

The next day, Bill worked for a neighboring farmer—who worked only negroes. All day the fields rang with laughter and song and flashing comebacks. Bill thoroughly enjoyed this day and when night came he had two dollars and fifty cents to have our boots half-soled and to buy two new chambray shirts in Flagstaff.

"Well," said Bill with satisfaction, "we have five jerked deer and fifty pounds of beans. Now to find a potato field."

"And a winter roof-tree," I added wryly.

LIVING OFF THE LAND

Flagstaff was hard hit by drought. There was one well, a rancher told us, where we might get water. It belonged to the Widow Jones, but "Don't say I sent you," he added hastily.

The Widow Jones was a big woman with a strict hairdo and fierce black eyes under heavy brows. "Who told you I have water?" she snapped. "If it was that no-good old tightwad, Dr. Thorne, he has water too, but you don't catch him giving any away. Well," she added self-righteously, "my neighbors can't say I ever turned anyone away thirsty. You can water your animals and make camp in my pasture—and wash your clothes." This last with a glance that scored a direct hit on my travel-stained Levis.

As we turned toward the well, she called, "Aren't you the folks that's headed for Mexico?"

Then I recognized her. She was the same woman who two days before had halted her pickup on the road and leaned toward us to shout, "Where you going?" Despairing of an explanation at such long distance, I had merely yelled back the farthest place that entered my head.

"How old are you?" she had shouted again.

"Thirty-three," I had screamed in weary exasperation. To which she had retorted loudly, "You look lots older. Just so weathered, I s'pose."

To this there was no comeback. I knew that by now my skin had practically the texture of those old heat-curled leather shoes that we used to find on the Death Valley dunes.

Camp made, I trotted up to visit. After days of silence I was always bubbling with eagerness to talk—woman-talk for a change. In a few moments the widow and I were as chummy as though we lived only a fence apart, and I was telling her the story of our trip. She was so fascinated that she hated to stop for dinner, she said, and why didn't I go down to camp and get my sourdough and make biscuits to go with her ham and fried potatoes? Her son must hear the whole story, too.

While Bill and the son were roaring with mirth in the living room, I helped the widow with the dishes. She put Clorox in the dishwater. "Just in case," I mused, with inward laughter.

"Those potatoes were wonderful," I purred contentedly, "first potatoes we've eaten for months."

"What do you eat?" she asked curiously.

"Jerky and sourdough," I answered. "But Bill worked in the bean harvest and now we have beans to last all winter."

"Well, our potatoes are about ready to dig," she offered. "I'm going to give you potatoes to take along. Now don't argue—you must have potatoes."

LIVING OFF THE LAND

There are people with whom you can't argue. It didn't seem reasonable that anyone would wish to *give* us our winter's supply of potatoes, but that's what she said, I told Bill later, and we'd better leave one burro empty to carry the added load.

In the morning we pulled up to her gate. "We're on our way," we shouted.

"Well, don't forget your potatoes," she called back and came out bearing a small brown paper bag which she handed to Bill. "I wouldn't sleep a wink if I'd forgot them," she said.

Bill took the bag. He peeked into it. Wordless, he handed it to me. I peeked. Inside were the potatoes destined to see us through the winter—two white and two sweet.

"Well," remarked Bill blithely as we jingled on towards Flagstaff, "we are all set for a long hard winter. We have jerky, beans— and four potatoes."

"Bill, how can you be so unconcerned?" I fretted. "See those great black storm clouds gathering? Winter has overtaken us— too soon."

All through Flagstaff and twenty miles beyond, angry black clouds scudded across a leaden sky in desperate endless pursuit. Then one morning we awoke to find that in the night they had turned and were scudding just as madly back again. By this time we had reached the drop-off into lovely Oak Creek Canyon, and in a few hours the world of storm and winter lay far above us. Down in the canyon the sun shone brightly, although crisp autumn leaves swirled from yellowing trees.

Far down the canyon we came to an apple orchard and the burros rushed to the fence and craned their necks, trying to nip the luscious red fruit from the low-hanging branches.

"Oh, Bill," I cried longingly, "have we got enough money left to buy a burro load of apples?"

"I'll go in and see how much they are," he replied. In a short time he was back, no apples in hand, I noted with disappointment. "They are only a cent a pound," said Bill, "but he wants me to work a day for them. He's short of help, he says."

Came the dawn, Bill reported for work and at night he came back for two burros to pack home his wages. Into my lap he tossed two very young carrots.

"What," I inquired, "am I supposed to do with this infinitesimal bit of fodder? And where did you get it?"

Bill grinned. "The farmer gave me those. After the apples were picked, he asked me to bunch carrots to finish out the day. He said to put just seven carrots—no more, no less—in each bunch. These two were left over and he said I could have 'em to take home. I threw them off to one side but he kept coming back and putting them beside my coat, and every time he came around, he'd remind me not to forget my carrots tonight. Said he couldn't stand for anything to go to waste."

"Well, eat them," I shrugged, "they won't even make a stew."

"I thought of that," replied Bill casually, and pulled from his pockets two runty tomatoes and one deformed green pepper which he had filched on the way home.

"Seems," I muttered, busily pounding jerky to go in the stew, "we have entered a country of small-scale farming."

WE OVERTAKE THE
DEPRESSION

For the next three days we peeled, cut and dried apples on the great creek-bank boulders—while winter crept nearer by the precious minute. In a few miles the creek had led us to the little settlement of Camp Verde. Bill needed a change of diet, he said, and he was fishing under the bridge for bonytails one day, when he heard the voice of the Law.

"What," demanded an angry game warden, "are you doing?"

"Fishing," replied Bill innocently, holding aloft a small fish by one thumb. "See?"

"I see all right," thundered the game warden. "Don't you know there's no fishing here?"

"Why, there's good fishing here," reproved Bill. "I've caught six already."

"I mean the stream is closed," bellowed the Law. "Can't you read? It says, 'NO FISHING', and I'll throw you in the can if you get tough with me."

BURRO BILL AND ME

"Do you mean that?" crooned Bill, dropping his gear to throw his arms around the poor man's choleric neck. "But just wait till I go and get my wife—she's been worrying about where she'd spend the winter. And I have six jackasses—you'll put them on pasture, won't you? Oh, boy," he bubbled, "am I glad I met you!"

"Aw, hell, go on and fish," snorted the game warden as he disentangled himself and stalked disgustedly across the bridge into Camp Verde.

Near our camp were two veterans living on a meager pension. "Why don't you go up to town Tuesday for Relief?"

"Explain to me," demanded Bill, "about this Relief."

"Shucks, everybody's on Relief," replied the veterans. "Once a week you go to the Relief office and they give you canned beef and fresh meat."

"You mean they give that kind of stuff away?" demanded Bill. "Why, the people on the Strip have to steal all their beef, eat illegal venison, and drink Mormon tea. This I must see!"

So for one day of the Great Depression, we were on Relief. It was enough. The canned meat was undoubtedly cut from the dying critters of the drought land, and the piece of fresh meat wrapped in newspaper proved to be something that I was never able to identify, but which resembled nothing so much as half of an unborn calf.

Now Bill's prediction was verified. With winter before us, he needed a job, and it came seeking him right at our campfire. We were picking out bits of edible fish from the hard structure of a mess of bonytails, when an old car stopped and a tubby little man with crafty, somnolent eyes alighted, almost tripping himself on all the extra yards of material in his oversized jeans which were turned up a good twelve inches at the bottom. "Want to go to work?" he asked, picking his teeth with a twig jerked from a creek-bank willow.

"What doing?" asked Bill.

"Packin' ore. Got a little gold mine up in the hills—need some burros to pack the ore down. Pretty steep trail. You could work in the mine on days there was no ore ready."

"Any place to live?" queried Bill.

"Sure—good little cabin right on the creek bank."

"I'll take it," said Bill. "We'll move in today."

Our new home was in the hills near Cottonwood, Arizona. It was built of old boxes, pieces of corrugated tin, bits of tar paper and canvas, and when it rained, as it often did that winter, the roof developed so many leaks that eventually there were twelve coffee cans hung on wires to the ceiling to catch the drips. The first time it rained we arose every hour to empty the cans, and at 4 A.M. it was again my turn. I crawled sleepily out of the crude bunk bed and stepped smack into a rushing torrent! In the night the creek had risen and made its way under one corner of the cabin, directly beneath the bed. From this point it flowed over the door sill and rejoined the creek roaring down the canyon. We lived, during rainy weather, on a small island of dirt floor which contained the three-legged wood stove and a dining table hinged to one wall.

The little man—"Baggy Britches" I privately called him—had decided to eat with us and generously announced that he would pay fifty cents a day toward the food. Then he proceeded to stock our shelf with jars of homemade jam sent by his wife, for which he charged thirty-five cents a jar. I soon discovered that his jam quota for breakfast, lunch and dinner consisted of exactly one 35-cent jar.

"Where," I demanded of Bill, "do we come out on this deal? Are you working for him or supporting him?"

"I haven't quite decided," Bill replied gaily, "but did I tell you why he wears such huge pants? He says he buys them that way on purpose so his wife gets all that extra material to put in her quilts."

"With such a man," I prophesied darkly, "I can see that you have a brilliant future in the mining game."

Burro Bill and friend. 1936.

MINING AND MAYGEE

We didn't last long with Baggy Britches. He hated to get up in the morning and puff up the long trail to the mine. At the least hint of a stormy day, he would lie abed and make excuses to himself and Bill that the trail was too slippery and dangerous for them to risk their necks for a few paltry dollars.

He was deathly afraid of the blasting and always gave Bill the job of detonating the caps, while he ran outside and hid quivering behind an inadequate cedar that clung to the slope. Every time a pebble rolled, he yelled, "Cave-in!" and dashed to safety. At the end of the first month, he had worked the mine only nineteen days and had consumed a great hole in our supply of jerky and dried apples. Fortunately, beans did not rest well in his little round stomach.

Nearby was another claim operated by a wizened old mining engineer and a bombastic Los Angeles promoter. They offered Bill three dollars a ton to pack their ore—if any—down the mountain to the road. These men had a pretty good shack built with the stockholders' funds but there was no place for us but the same old water-swept cabin on the creek. The promoter agreed to feed our burros but was aghast at the amount of grain and hay consumed by our six burros and four of his own. He tried rationing them until Bill growled through his bushy red beard, "I'll feed the burros—you just furnish the feed."

The man was half afraid of Bill, and even I, his ever-loving wife, had to admit that Bill bore a strong resemblance to Ivan the Terrible. When a man's face is covered by a red hair mattress, you must look to the eyes for his character, and the promoter was not accustomed to looking men in the eye.

The wizened partner volunteered to bring our groceries from Cottonwood once a week. The first time he did this, I went up to his cabin to carry home my share. I knocked, but as he was hard of hearing, I stood waiting a moment. The old man was carefully sorting eggs, mumbling to himself, "A big one for me—a little one for her, a big one for me—a little one for her—" but the cost I noticed was divided equally.

We bought from the local bootlegger half of a dressed pig, at seven cents a pound. The old man stopped by the bootlegger's and picked up our meat. When he delivered it, he said, smiling toothily and looking about as benevolent as the big bad wolf, "I took the liberty of cutting off about ten pounds of it for myself. I knew you wouldn't mind if I paid you just what it cost you." I unwrapped the pork. He had very efficiently sliced out the loin and the upper half of the ham, leaving us the shank, a hoof and a curly dangling tail.

This Depression-born mining scheme eventually folded, but not until Bill had overtaken the fleeing promoters and demanded his long overdue wages. He never told me what happened, but it seemed that half the residents of Cottonwood accompanied the trio to the bank to watch the strictly cash transaction that Bill insisted upon.

I doubt that the stockholders fared as well.

Across the hills, three miles by pack trail, was still another mining project, known as the New Broom. Its business was to sweep clean any little pickings left by previous owners in the search for gold. It was owned and operated by a couple known as Leonard and Myrtle, and a young man, Floyd, with Mom, his mother. These optimistic fledgling miners hailed from Downey, California, and they were the happiest group of people we had seen in many a day. When they undertook this uncertain Depression venture, they followed the timeworn advice of Benjamin Franklin, "Reduce your wants," and were happily stretching every grain of gold to cover the bare necessities of life.

Bill joined their little venture, and we moved over to their hillside to take up residence in the remains of an old house-car. The New Broom, diligently worked from sun to sun, yielded up some thirty-five dollar ore, and this the boys crushed and ran through a small stamp mill. Production was enough to pay off the bill at the general store in Cottonwood and to keep the mine out of debt.

I went to Cottonwood with the boys to establish credit for the New Broom. We entered the big barnlike structure that housed the general store. Here were shelves of groceries, cases of meat, counters of boots, shoes and overalls; crockery, hardware, mining tools, powder, caps and fuses. Here was fishing tackle, ammunition, and a complete stock of liquor—and weighing beans was the proprietor, big fat silent Jess Siler.

BURRO BILL AND ME

How he managed to keep going, no one knew. On his books were the unpaid accounts of hundreds of small shoestring miners, scattered through the hills from Jerome to Bumblebee. To establish credit a man had only to state the name of his claim and Jess saw to it that he had a month's grub, tools, powder, overalls, shoes, and a gallon of whiskey, to begin work. If the mine paid off and the miner paid up, Jess encouraged cash trade by a liberal cash discount. Other clerks filled the orders but the cash was paid only to Jess Siler. Picking up an itemized order, he would inquire from deep down in his triple chins, "Cash?" If the answer was affirmative, he ran down the list changing prices here and there, and when he reached the end he added up the total, and subtracted another overall ten per cent. Often times we knew that he could not even buy the goods at the price he asked. Especially was this true of the miner's staple—whiskey in gallon jugs.

No miner ever began his day, or ended it for that matter, without a generous slug from the gallon, purchased with the grub as matter-of-factly as the flour and beans. For this essential mining equipment Jess charged four dollars and seventy-five cents. "Would make it four," he'd growl, "but gotta pay the Federal tax."

To know Jess Siler was to forget all the greed, pettiness and chicanery in the world.

To amuse ourselves, Mom, Myrtle and I roamed the hills, gathered firewood, watched the boys at work—and cooked. The men, working such long hours, ate prodigious amounts of food and often they were forced to lay off from their labors and go in search of rabbits and deer to replenish our larder.

Floyd was a young daredevil, continually wringing his Mom's

heart with his hairbreadth escapes from trouble. Once he invited us over to a wonderful dinner of roast veal that Mom had cooked. In Arizona, you simply did not ask your host where he got his meat. But the answer came towards the end of the meal when a stray cow thrust her head in the cabin window and bawled a mournful "Moo-oo-ooo" right into the platter of veal.

++++++++++

One day the mail brought a letter. It was from San Francisco—an incongruously feminine missive, lavender tinted, perfumed, and written in a delicate backhand script. It was from Maygee, the ex-wife of an old friend. Maygee was the kind of woman about whom my mother would have had "her doubts." She was highly unconventional, but warm-hearted and generous, and we loved her. Excitement always rode on Maygee's trail—excitement and glamour and a kind of nostalgia for all the youth and beauty one had ever known in one's own life.

Now Maygee, at twenty-six, was about to be married for the fourth time. She was bringing her prospective groom for our approval, after which they were to be married in Yuma and go on to New York for a honeymoon. He had just won the "Irish Sweepstakes or something" and was, at least temporarily, "rolling in money."

Mom had gone back to the Coast and Floyd was boarding with us. It was dark when Maygee arrived and they found us at supper in the dim glow of a coal oil lamp. Maygee's man was just a man as far as I could see, but then, all men looked lustreless beside Maygee. Her face glowed brighter than the lamp, and above her big pansy eyes her bright-tinted hair shone too, with a golden aura.

Suddenly I saw Floyd staring at her and saw that Maygee knew he was staring and loved it. Then there was again that charged electric atmosphere that always I associated with Maygee and her conquests. Floyd was a dead duck. "Poor Floyd," I thought, "he's been out here so long alone—and now this has to happen."

Maygee worked fast. The next day she had sent her young man on to New York alone—and she was planning to make us an extended visit, if you please. "Oh Lord," I groaned, "Let her not hurt Floyd too much."

In a couple of days, Maygee climbed up to the mine to walk home with the boys. Bill and Leonard returned home on time but it was past dark when Floyd and Maygee came sauntering, hand in hand, down the winding trail. I was cooking supper. Maygee slipped over to me and whispered sweetly, "Do I look like the cat that swallowed the canary?"

I searched her face. "Did you?" I demanded.

"Yes," she confessed shamelessly. "We'll be married in three days—want to bet?"

"No," I replied shortly, "He hasn't got a chance."

In less than three days we all journeyed to Clarkdale to witness the ceremony. Maygee looked lovely in a pair of sailor pants left over from her third husband. Floyd never took his eyes from her face. "He takes it seriously," I mused.

And so, for a wonder, did Maygee. She settled down to become the world's best pioneer woman. She learned to chop wood, to cook on a wood stove the mealy rich salt pork and garlic-flavored frijoles so dear to the miner's heart, and to make light loaves of crusty bread. She learned to shoot, and on days that the mine was closed down, about the hills roamed the tall gorgeous girl and little happy-hearted Floyd, hunting a rabbit for their evening meal. As times grew tougher, Maygee grew more clever, and what she could devise out of a can of pink salmon or a hunk of tough venison, was amazing. It wasn't always easy and once I found her in a tantrum of fury, stamping underfoot a mass of recalcitrant pie dough that refused to hang together. "I'll learn to cook these damn pies if it kills me," she sobbed.

Maygee had a love of all the odd characters of the hills—a big, warm-hearted understanding that forgave them their faults, or rather, did not see them. She loved life, and she loved this husband—this manly little miner, hard-drinking, hard-working, hot tempered, but possessed of an innate integrity that Maygee had not found in her past experience with men. For all his small stature, Floyd was a man that a woman could lean on—and this Maygee did, for the first time in her restless, seeking life.

But Maygee's time was short. They had been married but a few short months when the car that Floyd was driving at top speed crashed into a telephone pole, and Maygee learned that her Arizona idyll was ended. Stunned, she stepped out of her denims and sweat shirt, back into the red suit with the trimming of fur that she had worn on that first spring night. Then with scarcely a farewell, Maygee went out of our lives. We never heard of her again. All we had left was her gilded shining memory and a little verse written in her delicate backhand script in our pocket volume of Robert Service—a whimsical, irreverant tribute to the miners she had met. It read:

> *"The mountaineers have hairy ears,*
> *They sleep without their britches;*
> *They chase the squaw-ers in their underdrawers,*
> *The hardy sonsabitches!"*

Lusty lovable, warm-hearted Maygee!

HIGH HOPES AND HARD LABOR

Full of enthusiasm for mining, we had promoted ourselves a small grubstake. It wasn't much—only thirty dollars a month, sent by a small group of doctors and nurses we had known in California. It was enough, however, to buy food, powder and fuse, and to pay for the necessary assays on our findings—should there be any. In return, the findings worth staking were to be shared fifty-fifty between Bill and our grubstakers. We were as enthused as they, sure that in the course of a few months we would turn up a nice little overlooked pocket of gold ore.

Among the miners there was talk of a primitive wilderness about sixty miles down the Verde River, called the Mazatals. This was the country that Zane Grey wrote of in *Under the Tonto Rim*, and if Zane Grey had been there, we reasoned, it must be primitive. Everywhere along our way, when we found ourselves far removed from civilization, pretty soon someone would recall "the time that Zane Grey came in here." He had gone lion hunting in

177

the Mazatals. No one had prospected there, said the miners, in the past thirty years, not since the Phelps-Dodge copper interests had combed it for new sources of copper ore. Copper and gold often went hand in hand and there was copper in stringers. Perhaps a man afoot, with plenty of time on his hands, could turn up one of those Arizona "blow-holes" and take out ten or twelve thousand in a matter of weeks. That's the way prospectors talk—never less than in thousands.

It's a contagious kind of talk and by midsummer we had reached the mouth of the East Verde and had climbed the ridge that separated us from the rugged brush country of the celebrated Mazatals. Below us lay mile on mile of chaparral, so dense that a man could almost walk on its stiff surface. The cattle and deer had wormed tunnels through it so that always they traveled under the surface of the brush, pushing their way with horns and antlers, unseen and unseeing. Below lay the thin silver trickle of the East Verde River, and to it we made our way, sometimes in the open, but more often in the chaparral tunnels of the animals. Not since ascending the mountain had we seen any sign of human occupation.

Now that we were here, how to start prospecting, when everywhere the eye met only the impenetrable thickets of chaparral? The Death Valley prospectors used to squint across miles of naked hills to see a "likely looking formation" or color that indicated mineralization. You couldn't squint two feet here except along the sycamore-lined river bank.

But where there are cattle there are inevitably cow-punchers and in a few days one showed up. He pointed out the trail we had missed and told us that the canyons sweeping down to the river

178

were clear of chaparral and connected by trails, so that a man might travel from canyon to canyon, and up and down their length, without setting foot in the dense brushland. This, he said, was a country of game—deer, fox, coon, coyote and many bear and cougar roamed almost unmolested in the dense wilderness. Six miles away lay his ranch and one other, and twelve miles farther on lay Payson, a small cattle town in the mountains.

A whole mountain all to ourselves! In imagination we returned to civilization bearing gold and silver, as we lay staring up through the white sycamore branches at a coldly knowing moon. "Another pair of amateurs expecting to beat the game," it leered, but Bill quoted happily, "It isn't the gold I'm wanting, so much as just finding the gold!"

For three months then, we fought our way up the Mazatals, plagued by swarming blow-flies so desperate to reproduce that they covered even the warm wet saddle-pads and our sweaty hat-bands with their loathsome eggs. At camp, there were not only these pests, but ants in such numbers that they nearly consumed an entire deer carcass in a single night. There were yellow jackets also to devour our meat, and in the water holes were myriads of dead bugs and wood-rats that had to be strained out.

Worst of all to me were the rattlers always lurking in the dark leaf mold of the shadiest places. Bill, himself, had just one fear and that was of rattlesnakes. He always led the way and kept a wary eye on every inch of ground before setting foot on it, but even then one time I did not halt fast enough at his urgent command and reached for a hand-hold just inches away from a coiled rattler. Slats had taken to wandering farther away from the trail and was little protection by day, but in camp one night she rustled

179

out two rattlers just ten feet from my cooking, and the following morning dug up still a third in the same spot. In the final six weeks of summer we killed thirty-six rattlers.

The game that we killed was a constant care. Yet even in summer, we were able to keep fresh meat as long as six weeks. The air was dry and the nights cool, and every night the meat was hung to chill and dry a thick protective crust over the outside. In the morning we arose before dawn and, beating the yellow jackets and blow-flies by a hair, wrapped the chunks of crusted meat in a canvas bag tied tight at the top, then in all our blankets to insulate it against the heat of the day. Meat cared for in this way kept fresh for weeks, ending up a trifle odorous at the bone but as tender and delicious as any artificially aged beef.

Some translucent red berries that grew on stiff gray bushes with holly-like leaves were new to us so we first tried them out on the burros. They ate them eagerly, so, relying on their good sense, we immediately ate some too and found them seedy with a tart delicious flavor. Our greatest luxury then became steamed puddings, sans eggs, but thickly dotted with berries and eaten with sugar, like the blueberry puddings Mother made in her native Nova Scotia years ago. The berries, we later discovered, were called "algerita" and the root was used by the Indians for the peculiar yellow dye of which they are so fond. The only other edible thing we could find was lamb's-quarter which made greens like spinach, but without flavor.

So our diet again was mainly venison. Bill had wrapped the inadequate 22 rifle around a boulder one day when it shot its exasperating left curve at two bucks locked in combat, and lost us some desperately needed meat. Undaunted, Bill came home with a wild pigeon, its throat precisely sliced by a 30-30 bullet. Pigeons are all right in summer, but when they go on their fall diet of acorns their flesh is as bitter as wormwood. Living off the country is fine if you have nothing else to do, but it takes every minute of a man's time to be constantly hunting, caring for the meat, and searching out scattered berries and caches of wild honey.

As prospectors, we were too busy for that. One day we knocked off a small piece of outcropping, and there in our hands was a solid chunk of the shiniest silver metal we had ever seen. To us, it looked exactly like the pure silver-lead galena we had seen in the Panamints, and here was a whole ledge exposed to sight—and how much underground? Hastily we sacked up a sample and trekked across the mountain to the ranch we had heard about, to have it mailed to the Arizona School of Mines for positive identification. For the next two weeks, we planned our mine. "Twenty pack mules," said Bill dreamily, "should pack out two tons each trip. Shall we write the grubstakers or wait and surprise them with the assay report?" Better wait, we decided.

And well we did. From the Arizona School of Mines came this terse report: "The sample submitted is of specular iron, valueless save in massive amounts, such as found in the Michigan iron mines." And from my father also came a note, "Scratch your mineral. If it streaks red behind the knife blade, it is specular iron. I saw mines of it in Nova Scotia." So much for that find. The red streak was there.

Our next discovery was barium, but of a low-grade impure quality. Then there were several small blow-holes that yielded up a color or two of gold dust when panned—and then came our next "big strike." On the very top of the Mazatals was a great

181

white quartz ledge. It was flecked with bits of copper pyrites, and the blue and green of azurite and malachite. Bill crushed some of the ore, panned it, and yelled excitedly for me. There, following the horn of the concentrates, was a half-inch string of dull yellow dust! We were rich!

All day we sat and panned, pan after pan, and always stringing far behind all the rest came this heavy fine yellow sand. Down the mountain again and off with another sample—this time to a Colorado assay company, and to double-check, one to Los Angeles.

Not one word of our discovery did we breathe to the rancher, although we were nearly bursting with our momentous news. Little did he dream that his ranch was to become headquarters for the biggest gold strike of the decade! The next two weeks were endless.

Then from Colorado came our report. Our sample assayed negligible amounts of copper and silver, but gold ran, to the ton, $121.76! At last, at last! Burro Bill had struck it rich!

This time we camped at the ranch and waited for the check report, though it did not matter now. In a week it arrived. It found our gold values to be the magnificent total of seventy-six cents per ton! Somehow we knew that this was right, and the other assay had been mixed up with someone else's ore. Yet, we sent still another sample and found eventually that our yellow "gold dust" was nothing but lead carbonates, and being the heaviest mineral present, it had naturally followed at the end of the panning. But as Bill said, "The thrill of thinking you've struck it is worth all the time and effort put into it, so let's try again."

HIGH HOPES AND HARD LABOR

One day we found a hole, overgrown with brush, where long years before someone had begun a prospect. The ore was red and crumbly and heavy with chunky bits of dull lead-colored metal. The next time we were out to the ranch, we sent off a sample and in due time found that this was silver-lead with a content of twenty-six dollars in silver to the ton of ore. Again we sacked up a specimen, this time twenty pounds, and sent it to the smelter at Clarkdale, seventy miles away. The smelter would take our ore in quantities, but the penalty on the lead would run the cost of smelting higher than the ore could stand, in addition to the heavy cost of mining and transportation. Our only hope lay in finding richer ore as we burrowed farther underground.

This chance we decided to take.

Burro Bill, Mrs. Bill, Balboa and pets offering their hospitality at Baker, California.

A dugout home in Baker, California. Steps led down into a cell, six feet wide and ten feet long with a door and one small window.

PELTS FOR PETS

Only two miles from our claim we stumbled onto the only cabin on the mountain, deserted these past few years, but still in good repair. In the gathering twilight, it was an eerie setting. Down the trail dry leaves rushed to meet us, whispering sadly of oncoming winter. Overhead, naked sycamores locked white arms and shuddered in a chill October wind that rattled the cabin windows and made a rhythmic knocker of a dry old deer hide, insecurely nailed against its door. Creeping through sycamore roots and piled dead leaves was an icy trickle of clear spring water, and across the narrow canyon we discovered another necessity of life—pile upon pile of corded wood in four-foot lengths, rotting away on top, but good oak and juniper beneath.

Bill was in raptures. "Aren't we the luckiest two people?" he marveled. "Shelter, water and fuel, all set and waiting for us. And the most picturesque spot since the days of Daniel Boone! I wouldn't trade places with all the millionaires in America right this minute!"

BURRO BILL AND ME

And neither, at that moment, would I, for already I had spied what my heart had longed for—a galvanized washtub. In Arizona cabins, three things were left if the owner intended to return—a stove, a broom, and a washtub. Immediately that dreary little cabin was *home*. Around that precious washtub centered all my woman's instinct for nesting, building and settling down. It was a symbol of the femininity so long discouraged in this world of animals and men. No longer was I just a part of a moving pack-string. I was a woman, the queen of a stove, a broom, and a washtub that belonged to me, and me alone. It was a wonderful feeling.

But my reigning hours were short. In between, I was Bill's "mucker" in the mine. Every morning we arose with the birds, ate a huge skillet of venison steaks and seven pan-sized hotcakes apiece, liberally smeared with thick Utah honey and washed down with quarts of black boiled coffee. Then we went out in the woods to cut green oak timbers and haul them on burros across the hills to the mine. The last steep pitch was agonizing effort for sturdy old John and big stiff-legged Blackie, and had to be accomplished foot by painful foot. Then the burros were taken down again and our day's work in the mine began.

Bill had gone out to Payson and bought drill steel, sledge hammer, caps, fuse, and all his mining needs. First he drilled the holes by the laborious hand process of slowly turning a short piece of drill steel against the hard rock, while hitting it with rhythmic blows from a four-pound single jack. When he had the holes in a "set" spaced to break the rock in the desired direction, he tamped in the dynamite, set the cap and fuse, yelled "Fire" to all nonexistent bystanders, and we scrambled to safety to watch her blow.

After the dust had cleared a little we re-entered the mine, "mucked" out the broken rock and rubble, peered anxiously at the face of the tunnel to see if the ore vein was still there, and proceeded to haul out the necessary tons of waste involved in the exposure of a mere stringer of ore. It was my job to push the waste rock over the slope and smooth the top down into a neat mining dump. That done, I helped Bill raise the heavy green timbers that he had already notched to fit together into a square arch, and to hold them up while he wedged them securely into place. Overhead, to retain the loose rubble, he built a neat riprap of small limbs laid close together. Bill was a meticulous worker, sparing no pains to make his tunnel smooth and trim to the eye as well as firm and secure from falling rock or a future cave-in. But digging a one-man mine is a slow process and one foot of tunnel a day was the best we could hope for. In a few months, we should be able to tell what the narrow silver vein intended to do—to widen out into a body of ore, to tilt up or down, or to disappear entirely.

"Couldn't a mining engineer tell which way it was headed without all this work?" I asked Bill.

He grunted. "Only God can predict the course of an ore vein. Never try to figure it out and take a short cut. That's why there are so many abandoned mining holes."

I saw what he meant, but apparently the grubstakers expected quick results. In the course of two or three months they had all become delinquent except one valiant old lady, sure to the end that

187

this prospect would make a mine. But her five dollars a month was hardly sufficient to sustain life and health in such a rigorous way of life, so we regretfully called off the whole deal, and turned our thought to the more immediate problem of how to eat.

One day Bill rode over to Taylor's ranch and came back with a pack burro heavily loaded with a grotesque pile of steel. "What in the world is that?" I cried, and then I saw—three dozen traps of assorted sizes.

"We are going trapping," announced Bill cheerfully. "I've got a catalog of fur prices, and with all the game in here we can clean up this winter. Here's the recipe for bait—it's a secret formula that some old trapper gave Dick Taylor, and he says it's so potent that even the deer come to it. Nothing can resist this scent-bait we are going to make."

He handed me a slip of paper. "Take a male coyote," I read, "remove all the glands, cut up, and pour over them a few ounces of male coyote urine. Add a few inches from the lower gut, a piece of the liver and bladder, and hang in an uncovered bottle for several weeks, or until it turns thick and black."

I gulped, "How," I asked meekly, "do we catch the male coyote to make bait out of him?"

"With a can of sardines," said Bill impatiently.

"Why not continue with sardines?" I queried helplessly.

"Because this is irresistible to *all* animals," and Bill began untangling traps and drags from the pile of rusted steel.

In due time the bait was made and brewing in a manzanita bush close by the shack. Bill was right. It was a potent scent. But why anything would desire to smell it at closer range than we were forced to, I could not fathom. "Looks to me like it would scare all the game out of the country," I commented.

"Animals have curiosity," said Bill witheringly.

Then one day the bait was ready and Bill went out to set his traps. He was gone all day. "I set them for five miles," he announced. "Now let's go down to the river and set coon traps. You just use shiny pieces of tin for them." Along the edge of the river Bill placed his traps in the water, the trigger set with a small piece cut from a tin can lid. "The coon sees it and dabbles his hand behind him, trying to grab it without looking at it," explained Bill. "Coon are easy to catch."

Bill waited until the next evening and rushed down to the river to look at his traps. After dark I heard him coming up the trail, talking to someone. The "someone" proved to be a very wet and shivering little coon, Bill's bootlace around his neck for a collar and a long stick tied to that for a leash. Bill was bringing home his fur afoot.

"See what I caught?" he said proudly. "Won't he make a wonderful pet? You know I walked up to this trap and at first I didn't see anything. Then I heard a funny pitiful little whimper, and there sitting on a rock in midstream was this cold wet little coon. When he saw me he put both little black hands over his eyes and peeked through his fingers to see what I was going to do. He was scared to death, and he sounded just like a scared baby. I could no more kill him than I could a baby either. Isn't he cute?"

From that time on, Ike, the coon, was part of the family. Bill made him a little tree house and by day he stayed aloft, but each night he came down to dance on the end of his chain and beg

corn and raisins. He loved to climb over us, industriously searching pockets, hatbands and Levi cuffs for the hidden food, but let
us so much as touch that beautiful electric fur and he would whirl
to attack.

He only glared balefully at the foxes, ring-tail cats, civets and
coyotes that soon were tied all around the cabin, hungrily awaiting the trapper's return each day. When the animals became so
numerous that Bill was forced to kill a deer to feed them, he sadly
gave up trapping and turned the booty loose.

"I guess I wasn't cut out to be a trapper," he confessed guiltily,
"I don't like to squash the life out of things, but I've had a lot of
fun getting acquainted with animals this winter."

The cow-puncher had been right. In the Mazatals Bill caught
(and fed through the winter) every kind of game save bear and
mountain lion. Thus far we had not seen a lion, although often we
came upon rocky ledges strong with their scent, and sometimes in
soft, sandy places we saw great cat tracks. As for bear, I had been
dreading them. The cabin bore huge scratches where one had
tried to claw his way in to a pan of wild honey. Always I felt that
some day that bear would get hungry and remember where he left
the honey. Once we saw him eating manzanita berries in a thicket
along our trail but he seemed only mildly curious at our presence,
and soon lumbered off with occasional backward glances at the
burros and their strange cargo.

With Bill's trapping such a dubious success, there was still the
old plaguing question of how to eat! This was solved for us—and
how!—by the receipt of a letter from friends on the Coast.

"Will you," they begged, "take a relative of ours, just out of
San Quentin? He has served a five-year term for robbery and isn't

dangerous—just weak and broken, and he needs the lift that Bill could give him in making a fresh start. We feel that such a life as you lead would be ideal for him. Will you take him for one-half of his pension which is forty dollars a month?"

Bill read the letter slowly and laid it aside. In his blue eyes was the old familiar light, that zeal to protect all weak and helpless things against the world. I knew his answer. Jim was to take the place of Bill's Indians, and of Slim in Death Valley, of Jack the sick burro he had tenderly brought back from death on the Arizona Strip, of the animals he had petted and cared for all winter. Jim was to be Bill's baby.

"Why, oh why," I wondered, "wasn't I a clinging vine? If you cling, inevitably you find support. And this Jim comes all the way from a stretch at San Quentin to find his—in Bill."

This time the advent of someone from the outer world filled me with a premonition akin to what Eve must have felt when she discovered the serpent in the Garden of Eden.

"The truck in which we went to New York!"

*Ishawipe, baby coyote, joined the family during
Heldorado Days, Las Vegas, Nevada.*

BILL'S BABY FROM THE BIG HOUSE

In due time, Jim reached the dirt road at Taylor's ranch and there we met him with a saddled burro to make the last lap of his journey to our camp. Not wishing to tell Mrs. Taylor that Jim was an ex-convict, we told her that he was a sick friend, coming to regain his health in the woods. This story was confirmed by one look at Jim's pallid face with its perpetual disturbing leer caused by a one-sided facial paralysis, and by his shuffling gait and stooped shoulders due to his constant effort to appear invisible. If she noticed his prison habit of holding his cigarette carefully hidden in the cup of his hand, like me she did not realize its significance, so revealing to those who have been "in stir."

Almost at once we realized that Jim was the most helpless adult we had ever encountered. From the moment that he dropped his duffel in his little tepee tent and came out with an air that seemed to say, "Well, here I am—here's your baby," he had to be watched and tended like a toddling child.

BURRO BILL AND ME

Over and over we showed him how to saddle and mount a burro but the knowledge did not penetrate his mind in the least. He was forever asking questions about my kitchen chores. One day when he jerked up suddenly to inquire with apparent eagerness, "Edna, tell me, do you fry eggs in grease or water?" Bill's patience was exhausted. More and more, he took to leaving the care of Jim to me, while he resumed the mining chores alone.

One morning Jim dashed in and gasped, "Edna, fix me some breakfast and pack me a lunch, saddle me a burro and find my gun. There's a buck about two miles away and I bet my brother-in-law that I'd shoot the first deer I ever saw with the first bullet I ever fired. Hurry, will you?"

"Jim," I explained patiently as I dished up venison steaks, "deer do not sit down and wait two hours for the hunter to go home for his gun. That buck is ten miles away by now. And it is exceedingly unlikely that anyone could hit the first deer he ever saw, outside of a zoo, with the first rifle shot he ever fired."

But Jim was undaunted, so I caught and saddled his burro, helped him get his feet in the right places, handed him his gun and lunch, and wished him luck.

Two hours later I was at the mine—and there was Jim weary but triumphant, leering proudly at a mangled bloody deer head which he had placed in the wheelbarrow of rocks. "I did it!" he announced. "I won that dollar off my brother-in-law. I killed the first deer I ever saw with the first shot I ever fired!"

I looked at Bill and he, nodding confirmation, whispered, "Don't tell Jim, but see why he was able to do that? That buck's neck is swollen as big as his body. He's in rut and when you catch a buck and doe together at that time, their minds are not on hunters. Jim just intruded at a very opportune moment but the meat isn't fit to eat. He'll never know the difference though, so don't spoil his fun by telling him."

After this episode with the lovelorn buck Jim was eager to see a bear, and one day his wish was gratified. He topped a little ridge and came face to face with a small brown bear. Jim retreated backward into Bill's arms and stood frozen in his tracks, mumbling over and over in complete bewilderment, "Bill, there's a bear. . . . Bill, there's a bear. . . . Bill . . ."

"Well, shoot it!" said Bill impatiently.

"Bill, it's a *bear!*" Jim repeated, and throwing down his rifle, he fled. Fortunately, so did the bear.

It wasn't long after this that Bill and Jim went off on a six-day hunting trip, leaving me with only the coon for company. They even took Slats. At first I enjoyed surcease from Jim's eternal questions, but as night came on in the little canyon the full awareness of my isolation came over me. The boys were six miles down the river. Suppose the bear came back for our honey? Bill had half the blankets and I was cold. I tossed until 2 a.m., haunted by visions of bears ripping loose boards from the cabin in search of food.

At last I dozed off, but the next moment I was wide awake and shivering with fright. On the wooden doorstep—heavy footfalls! The door flew open and on the hollow floor there was the sound of heavy feet, and a great bang as the burros' feedsack was upset!

My heart flew into my throat and stuck! I could not scream, and if I did, who was to hear me? Timidly, fearfully, I groped for the flashlight under my pillow, and hoping to frighten the intruder away I flashed a beam directly upon his huge black carcass. He jerked up his head and stared into the light, and as I saw his long droopy ears, my heart gave a relieved thump and slid back into place.

In the dark alone, I laughed out loud. The "bear" was an old black stray burro who had smelled the sack of corn and pushed his way in to a good feed. I led him outside and, comforted by a familiar presence, went back to bed and fell into a sound sleep.

By the time the boys returned, Bill was weary, reporting that Jim had been even more helpless than usual. When they camped in rocky woodless areas, he burned all the fuel in one big blaze. The next night, surrounded by timber, he froze over a tiny fire wailing, "You *told* me to build a little fire and save wood!" He lay in bed late and asked Bill to leave his breakfast. Bill wrote down a recipe for hotcakes and left it on the pack boxes. At night, he returned to a hungry and disgruntled Jim. "I'm starved," he grumbled. "Look at your damn recipe!" pointing to a crumbling burnt mass of flour and grease spattered against a tree trunk.

Bill looked at it and light dawned. He had carefully written down the ingredients, thinking that anyone would know enough to add water to make a batter, but he reckoned without Jim. Jim assembled the ingredients as listed and dumped them in the skillet. The force with which it had spattered about told the results.

A few days later, Bill and Jim went into Payson for supplies. Jim's purchases, we soon discovered, consisted of several gallon jugs of wine. He hid them in the brush and made frequent forays toward them, growing more and more belligerent with each trip. I was heating wash water over an outdoor fire when Jim conceived the idea that it would be amusing to drag the coon through the hot coals. Poor little Ike spit and hissed in helpless fury and Jim laughed in drunken glee. Helpless to stop him, I ran for Bill. He took one look and, grabbing the coon from Jim, said in a deadly cold voice that I had never heard before, "Jim, if you ever do that again, I'll kill you like the snake you are."

Jim's face contorted with fury. He ran to his tent and returned with his rifle. Ramming it into Bill's stomach, he shrieked in a high hysterical voice that sounded unreal and melodramatic there in the calm woods, "Bill, say your prayers—I'm going to kill you!"

I stood frozen, powerless to stop the shot that would send my husband's blood spilling out onto the dry leaves. Then my heart gave a great leap of relief and pride in Bill. With his life balanced on an unsteady finger, he was not afraid. He looked Jim squarely, sternly in the eye, compelling the obedience that is second nature to prison men. "Lay down your gun, Jim. Give me your shells. Now go to your tent. Don't come out until I tell you. You can't have wine and a gun, too—take your choice."

Jim began to cry. "You take the gun, Bill," he sobbed, "but leave me a drink. I need it."

This incident left me apprehensive and shaken. I wanted Jim to go but Bill shrugged, "He'll be all right now. He may never go berserk again, but I'll keep his gun a while."

On the next trip, I went with Bill to Payson. Jim was dismayed at being left alone all day. "Let me have my gun, Bill," he begged, "so I can shoot some quail. I can't sit alone all day with nothing to do." Bill gave in.

When we returned, down the trail sitting on a big rock we saw Jim, gun across his knees and a gallon jug beside him.

"He needs a lesson," said Bill. "I'm going to have a little fun with him." And drawing a bead on the rock, Bill let fly with a

30-30 bullet, kicking up rocks and dirt in every direction, and sending Jim at a long gallop, screaming, "Bill, I didn't shoot, I didn't drink, I didn't do *anything!*"

Bill was ashamed. "Now that just goes to show you," he said soberly to me, "that living out like this makes a man about half-wild. Can you imagine me thinking it would be funny to shoot the rock out from under a man? In a civilized country they put people in jail for things like that. Out here, it's just considered legitimate primitive fun. I guess the time has come for Jim to go—and for us, too."

OUR NEW HOME— 750 MILES AWAY

Having completely closed the door on our former way of life, we felt no desire to return to that phase of our existence. If at times I thought with longing of the comforts enjoyed by even the poorest city-dweller—soft beds with springs, bathtubs, water running from taps at the touch of a hand, heat that came from some unseen source that only the janitor knew—it was a longing for something remote, like a Cadillac or a million dollars.

The thought of return brought only Death Valley to mind, for there we had put forth roots of a sort; there were beloved friends and neighbors among the prospectors and Indians. On a map we traced the new National Monument boundaries and found that they did not extend to Baker, a little settlement in the Y of two highways, where travelers passed east to Las Vegas and north to Death Valley. Bill picked this spot, sight unseen, for our future home. Where tourists stopped, Bill knew he could make a living. "We'll figure how when we get there," he added airily.

BURRO BILL AND ME

Preparations for this new adventure were simple. First, we turned out four burros to end their days on the banks of the East Verde. They had earned a rest. With us we planned to take Balboa, the striking black and white burro that we had caught and tamed, and little Jack, never happy away from his Death Valley home. According to the Indians, he was now thirty-three years of age, and we wanted him to end his life in familiar haunts.

There was little else to do but roll the hard thin mattress tightly, cover it with canvas to keep the birds from nesting in it, and swing it by wires from the rafters, that the mice might not use it for a warm winter home. This much we owed to the next occupant, as well as the covered can each of coffee, sugar, flour, salt, baking powder and a small can of bacon grease left on the shelf. Ike, the coon, had been turned loose to follow the call of spring. There was nothing to do but hang up the washtub, secure the cabin door, and start walking—seven hundred and fifty miles—to Baker, California.

It was June when we stopped for the last time at Taylor's ranch. Once a week, for months, we had spent a few hours with the Taylors, growing more and more attached to this fine family. Mrs. Taylor had known every privation that a woman can suffer, and her heart was as big as the country that bred her. Thirty years she had lived in this two-room log house with its simple furniture of two double beds, two straight chairs, a plank table and benches, and the pride and joy of the household—a huge wood range where a pot of red beans simmered 365 days of the year. Five times in her first years there, she had made her bed in the woodshed to bear, alone and unaided, the children that were today among the finest young people in the countryside. She alone knew the loneliness that was often mine, of one woman in a womanless world.

Her husband, Dick, was a man of few words, having that rare ability to sit through long silences in complete ease. Yet just now, he was being most articulate on a subject dear to the heart of every stockman in the West. What was the Roosevelt administration going to do for the drouth sufferers, and what of the bitterly debated Taylor Grazing Act? Having just passed a great pile of dead cattle out on Dick's range, each bearing a bullet hole through the head, we were eager to know about this mass slaughter of worthless beef.

"The government pays nine dollars a head if the cattle can't make the railhead," explained Dick. "It is doubled if they are accepted by the government inspectors for shipping, and them ol' cowboys are sure twisting the tails off them ol' critters to get the last few steps out of them. But what chance has the stockman got against a lot of puddin' heads out of Washington that never saw a damn critter except in pictures? You won't believe this, Bill, but I swear it happened.

"We thought the inspector we had wasn't passing enough cattle, so we asked Washington to replace him. In a few days, here comes a serious young feller in a nice suit of clothes, and perched hisself up on the corral fence. For three days he just sat there and watched them ol' longhorns, muleys, bulls, heifers and every kind of critter go past, and never said a word. We all say to ourselves, 'Now there's a man that knows his business.' The third day, he went to lunch with me and he asked real polite and earnest-like, 'Mr. Taylor, tell me. I've been watching these cattle and I notice that some of them have horns and some don't. Now, tell me, Mr. Taylor, is it a result of the drouth that they didn't all shed their antlers at the same time this year?' And that," concluded Dick grimly, "is what is wrong with the drouth relief and the Taylor Grazing Act and the whole damn government program."

Bit by bit, we wormed from Dick the story of his struggle to build up his threatened herd. "Most of us in here," he said, "got our start catching up the wild cattle of the Mazatals—"

"Wild cattle?" we queried, "How come?"

"Well, there was an old feller died and the bank come in and picked up the five thousand he paid taxes on, but the old man hadn't had a roundup for ten-twelve years and they was thousands with not a brand nor an ear-mark on 'em. Just mavericks. Stockmen figured he had at least twenty-five thousand head running wild all up and down this river, and clear to the Verde, over the mountain. So, people started movin' in and catching and branding the critters, and that was the start of nearly all the ranches around here. I been digging out them ol' moss-backs for years and there's still some left up in that brush country you been hiking in. A man never sees 'em, but you can hear 'em crashing through those brush tunnels sometimes."

"The way we brought the critters in," reminisced Dick, "was this. If I do say it myself, my boys are the ropinest fools that ever lived and they'd drop a noose plumb around a clump of bushes and right over the head of an old critter hiding out on the other side. Then we'd snub the ol' fool to a tree by the horns till she made 'em sore a 'fightin' to get loose, and when she learned not to fight, we snubbed her to an old jenny and turned 'em loose. You know how an old jenny is—nothing this side of hell can keep her from going home no matter how long it takes, and in a few days she'd always manage to drag the old cow into camp. But some of them old mossy-backs we caught just stood in that corral out there and stared back at them brush hills till they starved to death. Just died of a broken heart, I reckon."

"No wonder your boys made the big-time rodeo circuits," I commented, "with that kind of training."

"Yeah, my boy Bill just come back from Madison Square Garden," replied Dick. "He says the people back there are plumb wild—almost clawed the shirt off his back for souvenirs. Asked the damnedest questions, too. One woman asked him, 'Cowboy, what do you wear *under* them saddle pants?' She said they fit so tight she couldn't see how he set down. I reckon Bill was glad to get back home where people are civilized."

Some miles above Dick's ranch towered the gray stone battlements of the Mogollon escarpment, that sheer wall over which the Apaches were once driven by mounted U.S. soldiers on their ill-fated "Trail of Tears" toward their imprisonment in the stockades of Fort Sill, Oklahoma. The story has two sides; one I have read in my white man's history, the other we heard from an old Indian who had trod this trail on bare brown feet, chained to other toiling naked feet that changed each time starvation, thirst or zero weather struck close beside him. After a lapse of sixty years, there was in this old Indian's heart no love for his white brothers.

From the town of Pine our trail wound up the Mogollon Rim, higher and higher, until at nightfall we found ourselves in the infinite quiet of a tall pine forest. We made our camp on a small grassy knoll and turned the burros out to graze. In a few moments Jack and Balboa came hopping back on their hobbled forefeet, bells clanging wildly, eyeballs rolling in terror.

"Something's happened," said Bill. "They want help."

Then we noticed that their chests were covered with oozing drops of blood and over each droplet hovered the most enormous black gnats we had ever seen. The burros were almost insane from fright and pain. Bill got out the indispensable flyspray and flitted them thoroughly, at which they kicked up their heels in a gesture of thanks and returned to their grazing.

"That," remarked Bill tenderly, "is what makes the little bastards so damn lovable—their complete dependence upon us."

I forebore reminding him of all the times the "little bastards" had wedged themselves and their packs into cool mining tunnels in the heat of the day, and kept us kicked back into the scorching sun until our tongues hung out for the water they carried on their loaded backs.

It was on this little knoll next morning that I had one of the thrills of my life. Face to face, I met my first mountain lion.

A COUGAR AND
A COWPOKE

With the first beam of light I was wide awake, with the uneasy feeling that something was looking me over. Cautiously I pulled the covers down an inch and looked straight into the yellow eyes of a great cat face, not ten feet from the foot of our bed. The lion came a curious step nearer and his massive shoulders were in full view. I let out one terrible, terrified scream, "Bill, shoot it, shoot it!" and covered up my head. Slats set up a furious barking. No shot forthcoming, I peeked out and saw Slats' tiny black figure hard on the heels of the huge tawny cat. My heart sank. One blow from the great paw and Slats would be crushed to a pulp.

"Bill," I screamed again. "Shoot it, shoot it!"

Bill sat up, rubbed his eyes and yawned. "What's going on anyhow?" he demanded. Just then he saw the cat.

"A baby elk! A baby elk! My God it's a MOUNTAIN LION!" he bellowed. "Where's my gun?" But the lion had disappeared over the rim of the Mogollon escarpment.

BURRO BILL AND ME

Somewhat shaken, I started the fire and dabbed my hands in
the inch of wash water in the bottom of the gold-pan that we
allowed ourselves in these "dry camps." Bill was trying to pick up
the lion's tracks and figure out why he had come so close to us.
"The wind was with him," he concluded, "and he was as surprised
to see you as you were to see him. Lions don't walk right into
people that way. I've heard they are the biggest cowards on earth.
But I don't blame you for yelling—if I'd woke up and seen that
old cat looking me right in the eye, I'd probably have yelled
louder'n you."

"You did," I retorted dryly. "You scared the lion clear out of
this country."

We were now traveling on those by-ways where the real West
moves, unseen, unguessed by motorists on the highways. These
were the stock trails, narrowing to mere yards, widening to miles,
traversing the great national forests and grasslands, their boundaries marked by yellow signs in English and Spanish, nailed to
trees at intervals. Along these trails were feed, water and the
camps of herders on the move. At the sheep camps we liked to
stop and chat with the Basque herders and eat a meal of mutton
and bread baked in the pits of embers left from their evening fires.
In the cow camps we found the American punchers less eager to
talk and not nearly so hospitable. The "Bascos" usually had
burros to pack their camps and between burro-men there is the
same comradeship that exists between horsemen.

Once we came upon the "mother" camp of one of Arizona's
largest sheep outfits, and were charmed by its Old World atmosphere. The "major-domo," the "pastorals" and "caparals" were
all Basque, and life with them took on the leisurely unhurried

pace of their native Pyrenees. The buildings were rambling and weathered. In the kitchen, the major-domo's attractive American wife was teaching orphan lambs or "dogies" to nurse on a baby's bottle, and older lambs were romping and frisking up and down the steps. The sheep were the center of all being, and no attempt was made to minimize their importance. It is for this attitude toward his charges that the Basque is famous, and, in Arizona, he is the preferred tender of the flocks. The major-domo insisted on opening his storeroom, laden with tons of food awaiting distribution among the outlying camps, and piling on our burros rice, oatmeal, flour and raisins until we called a halt, protesting that we had no room to carry more. It reminded us of the stories of earlier-day Californians who kept a sack of gold coins in their guest rooms, and horses ready for the traveler with a tired mount. Yet just a few short miles away on the Flagstaff-Williams highway were tourists looking in vain for even so much as a mounted cowhand.

What a tourist would have given to have met Speedy! We found him in Long Valley. No sooner had we made camp than a tiny forlorn figure drifted in and proffered us a sack of wieners and candy bars. "Kin I eat with you?" he begged in a wistful little voice. Assured that he was welcome, the little figure settled blissfully against a log and waited for his supper.

Out of the tail of my eye, I studied this strange apparition that had drifted in out of the night. He was no more than five foot two, thin, dried, with an enormous old black Stetson riding like an oversized mushroom atop his protruding ears and shadowing his strangely old-man face. His Levis were tiny as was his checked shirt, but his dainty little cowboy boots were mere elfin stuff. He was a gnome in cowboy clothing, a wistful, heart-breaking little gnome. He caught my glance at his little boots and chuckled, "Made to order—can't get 'em small enough. Dancing, I wear little girls' patent leather Mary Jane pumps."

He ate so little that I suspected this was his way of getting acquainted. After supper, we sat by the fire and the little man said, "Call me Speedy—that's all the name I use."

Then Speedy went into his act. For four solid hours he put on a show, with story after story acted out in detail in his own inimitable manner. Speedy galloped at top speed around the campfire, reined in his phantom horse, humped over imaginary saddles, tossed off invisible drinks, and kept us roaring till our sides ached. Speedy was terrific. Speedy belonged in Hollywood. Speedy thought so, too. He promised to meet us there, should we ever get that far.

A week later we met him in Flagstaff. His face was swollen and blue and he had no teeth. "Had a toothache," he chuckled, "and the doc thaid he had to pull theven teeth. Didn't have any money, tho I took a thtiff drink, got off the train and yelled to the crowd, 'I kin lick any man here!' A big ol' boy thoved hith way up to me, and theth, 'Tzat tho?' and hauled off and knockth all my teeth out. I thaved twenty-one dollarth on that deal, hot thiggety thig!"

SEVEN DOLLARS BUYS
A BUSINESS

Now we came out on the highway leading toward Williams and we met the tourist on his own ground.

Tourists are funny people. When they get away from their accustomed surroundings and the restraining influence of home, they sometimes do the oddest things. A favorite stunt was to stop their cars ahead of us, while Papa or Junior jumped out and waited with camera poised to catch us head-on. The shutter would click and without a word to us the photographer would jump back in his car and roar away with his prize shot of the strange fauna he had just encountered.

At first this was funny; then it grew annoying. Bill hated rudeness. "It wouldn't hurt them to speak," he grumbled, "and ask if we minded their taking a picture of the *burros*. They could slip in a shot of us without being so obvious about it."

I laughed. "Don't you remember the woman in the tomato-colored slacks, mountain boots and Sunday-go-to-meeting hat, who walked up to me and purred, 'My deah, may I take your picture? You are so *quaint!*' and I so nobly refrained from purring back, 'And may I have *yours,* dear?' "

Not all tourists were like this. Some graciously asked permission to photograph our pack-string. To these Bill always said, sweeping off his broad-brimmed flat-topped Mormon hat, "Wouldn't you like to stand by the burros and let me take *your* picture?" This never failed to surprise and delight the traveler, his surprise being occasioned by the fact that Bill knew how to operate the Rolliflexes and Contaxes.

Bill was an amateur snapshot hound. And it was this that settled his future for him.

We had made our camp on a little hill overlooking the junction where hung a large sign, "57 MILES TO THE GRAND CANYON." Tourists kept stopping and asking for pictures or just taking pictures without asking. The nicest ones we asked to dinner and never had I seen people enjoy food as these Easterners did our frijoles and Dutch oven corn bread. There was one family traveling in a big antiquated house trailer with an observation platform in the rear. Bill was intrigued and they invited us inside.

After a while the man said, "I have something that you should have. It would be just the thing for you." And he brought out a large black box and a wooden tripod.

"A tintype camera," he explained. "We bought it to make expenses as we traveled, but we just aren't the type to meet the public. You have the gift of meeting people and I know you could sell tintypes of people mounted on that spotted jackass. Why, your fortune would be made, man! You could go anywhere and carry your meal ticket right with you."

SEVEN DOLLARS BUYS A BUSINESS

"How does it work?" asked Bill, and in a few moments he had seen a demonstration. "Here's your card, painted with a photosensitized film. Now you place it in this holder in front of your lens, snap the shutter, reach in through this black cloth sleeve, take your card in the thumb and forefinger, drop it through a slot into this tank of developer, fixer, and bleach, all in one. Leave it one minute, turn your tank and remove the finished picture, which is positive-direct, with a pair of tweezers, thoroughly wash the print, and hand it to the customer. 'Your picture while you wait.'"

Bill was entranced. "How much do you want for it?"

"Seven dollars, and I'll throw in two hundred cards and frames."

Carefully Bill counted out his money. There was seven dollars and some cents. Without a qualm, he handed over the money and took the camera. "Just like Jack in the Beanstalk fable," I thought.

That night Bill used up several films practicing taking pictures of the campfire. The next day he saddled Balboa with the McClellan riding saddle that we now used to pack our bed-roll, in place of the regular cross-tree pack saddle. He took the camera, the tripod, Balboa, and a sign we had made, "YOUR PICTURE ON THE BURRO," and went out to his place beneath the Grand Canyon sign. With a seven dollar camera, a wild jackass, and the whole world for a shop, Bill was in business. In two days, he had back his investment, and our books were in the black.

For six weeks we camped on the little hill, and every day at 2 P.M. came a warning little cloud to send Bill back to camp for the inevitable shower which meant that our water supply in the roadside ditches was secured for another twenty-four hours. Mornings the sun shone and Bill prospered. And life was good.

211

"Camping in sight of New York. 1938."

WE "MUG" OUR WAY
TO BAKER

Despite its apparent simplicity, the tintype camera was constantly springing new surprises. Once all the cards returned shining black blanks, while Bill, sweating nervously, poked desperately through the black sleeve, and tourist after tourist grew tired of waiting and departed. Finally, Bill sent me to camp for a blanket under which he opened up the machine and discovered a card stuck in front of the lens. With a sigh of relief he resumed business.

Soon a woman dismounted from the burro, seized her still-wet photo and demanded, "Where's the burro I was sitting on?" Bill gave a hasty glance and gulped. There were her head and shoulders over a murky purple sea. Fearful of losing the next customer who already had one foot in the stirrup, Bill hustled her off with the airy assurance, "The b-b-burro, madam, will come in later!"

Sometimes the customers wore strange white halos, and again sunbursts of light radiated from white clothing. Sometimes the cards were green and sometimes so dark that the white spots on the burro were the only things visible. Lacking any literature on the machine, Bill was in a quandary. There was nothing to do but experiment, hour after long hour, in different lights with different amounts of bleach, and at different distances, until the perfect formula was found for never-fail photos. Time was precious. In one minute from the time a customer mounted the burro, the picture must be done and in his hand or he would impatiently be on his way. One minute is a long time to a tourist bent on seeing the United States and half of Canada in two weeks!

One morning Bill awoke shivering and declared, "I feel winter. We haven't much time to get off this mountain." Hurriedly, we packed and cut across the forest to Ashfork, sleet-laced winds hard on our heels. Just out of Ashfork we killed our last deer. Bill shot it at 6 P.M. and while the carcass was still hot we sliced and hung it on oak bushes to dry. All night a stiff desert wind swept across the miles of open grassland, and by noon the next day our entire deer was dried into hard little chips of jerky that fitted into a twenty-five-pound flour sack.

In Ashfork at dusk we ran into a sheep-herder going to Oatman with a stock truck. He offered to load our burros and take us the next 150 miles, thus saving us eight or ten days of precious time. Loading the burros was nearly as bad as crossing the Grand Canyon bridge, but the sheep-herder was used to obstinate minded burros. There was only one choice for them and that was ahead, up the cleated tail-gate. For the next five hours Jack and Balboa squatted miserably on their haunches, necks stretched to the limit, eyes rolling in abject fear, as the truck swooped through hundreds of Arizona road-dips like a roller coaster on the down grade. When we unloaded near the Colorado River bottoms, they were staggering drunkenly from the fast pace of civilization.

We were hurrying now to cross the Providence Range before snow fell. Through the mountain passes fierce winds swirled and beat about us, biting through thin unlined jackets, turning our feet to lifeless lumps of ice and our hands to black-cracked smarting stumps. At night our wash water froze in the shallow gold-pan almost before we finished washing, right beside our little fire in the lee of rocky cliffs. Having only five blankets, we built a fire, raked it away, and put one blanket on a pile of brush laid on the warm ground. The other four we laid over us and kept snug and warm. The next day was worse than the one before.

It was the kind of weather that sends men and animals alike to seek shelter from winds that tore and raged and battered, chilling us to the very marrow.

Our food was once more exhausted, save for the dried deer meat. I was hungry. Slats, running along ahead, stopped and began to gulp something. I stared. It was a doughnut—a fresh sugary doughnut! I ran to her and grabbed the paper sack she had found. In it were still eleven beautiful doughnuts. Beside it lay another white paper sack. I tore it open. There were a dozen fresh cin- namon rolls, a loaf of wonderful white bread and a chunk of golden cheddar cheese! I looked around. Where had it come from? In that searing wind, it could have been there but a matter of moments. There was no car in sight and none had passed us. The sacks lay not on the highway, but on the dim old road that we were following some yards away, and parallel to the highway. Promptly we sat down by the roadside and ate the whole busi- ness, save for Slats' rightful share of the spoils. The mystery was never solved—to this day we still wonder how this fresh bakery food found its way sixty miles from the nearest bakeshop to the dim old unused road across the desert. Perhaps some old retired burro-tramp had seen us and sneaked across the desert to lay it in our path, knowing in his own heart the hunger that must be ours for the foods of a civilized world. We swore that should the time ever come when we again traveled the highways on wheels, we would never pass up a burro-man without giving him something baked. "A pie," I said dreamily, "I want to give every burro-man I ever meet a pie."

At Kelso, we took on supplies and found that Baker lay just across another small range. There was no road or trail, but once we gained the summit, Baker could be seen in the white alkali sink below. Thirty-six miles away, just twelve merciless hours of walking; and on Armistice Day 1936 we stumbled wearily into Baker.

There wasn't much to Baker. Just a cluster of white stucco gas stations, tourist cabins and cafes, in exact replica of desert towns for hundreds of miles in every direction. Out behind, squatting in dry desert silt, carefully hidden from the eyes of the tourist by a line of feather-plumed athel trees, were the shacks and tents of those who served the passersby.

A rheumy-eyed old man came limping excitedly to meet us. "By God," he roared, "I never expected to see the day that two young people had the guts to hike across them mountains. In twelve hours, you say? I want to shake your hands, young folks—"

"But that was nothing," protested Bill. "We've come fifteen hundred miles in the past two years."

At this the old man bellowed in a mighty voice, "All you people come here and meet two people with guts! I thought all the people with guts were dead or too old to do a gol-durned thing!" Excitedly, he hustled us around to meet the townsfolk who by now had turned out en masse.

The old man, we discovered, was "Uncle Brooks," eldest brother of that famous old desert character, "Dad" Fairbanks. Most of Baker was composed of Dad's relatives and descendants. It was a mighty clan and they took us to their hearts.

One of Dad's daughters, Betty, a big honest straightforward woman, said, "There's only one place to live. It isn't much but I've lived in a sight worse and you probably have too. Come, I'll show you."

Out behind the twenty little pale blue cabins of Dad's Tourist Court, the desert stretched bare and baked, cracked in great fissures by the sun. A deep ditch was the bed of the dry Mojave River. On its edge was a dugout, a hole dug out of the adobe bank, roofed over with old railroad ties. Steps had been cut from the dirt down into its dark depths. It was a dirt cell, six feet wide and ten feet long with a door and one small window. I was dismayed.

"Do people live in places like this?" I asked.

"They certainly do," replied Betty heartily. "This will be snapped up by the next prospector in for the winter if you don't grab it."

Bill nudged me that "Wife, shut-up" nudge and we moved in. He got permission to set up in business in front of Failing's Cafe and returned to his tintyping.

As an assistant I was worthless. Bill wanted me to get the

217

tourists safely on and off Balboa, put Jack's lead rope in their hands, and pose them as though they were setting out across the desert on a prospecting trip. I was to see that in the background there was nothing but the stretching desert wastes, and when the picture was snapped, I was to engage the tourist in interesting conversation while Bill finished the picture.

This I simply could not do. Naturally shy, my years away from people had made me even more retiring, and conversation with city-bred folks was an agony. I couldn't think of a thing to say to them, and they looked so queer to me. The knowledge that they felt the same about me was small consolation.

I spent my time roaming over Baker's extensive dump, collecting odds and ends to set up housekeeping. Had we reached the end of our journey only to come to this! If this was getting back to civilization, I preferred the cool clean forests, unsoiled by man and his refuse dumps.

CHRISTMAS COMES
TO BINNEY

Searching the dump one day for something that would serve as chairs, I heard a rasping cough. There on a pile of rags in the shelter of an old car body lay a thin little birdlike man, coughing as though his lungs would burst. I hurried to his side. "Why you have pneumonia!" I exclaimed as I saw the dark red flush high on one wasted cheek and the flaring of his pinched nostrils with each labored breath.

"Yeah, guess I'm done for," panted the little man.

I ran for Bill, my prop in time of trouble. "There's a man on the dump dying of pneumonia," I gasped. "What shall we do?"

"Take care of him, of course," was the prompt response.

Together we carried the wasted little figure to the shed where we kept our burros, and laid him in the clean straw. So long had we fought our own battles and settled our own affairs, that it did not occur to us that there were county hospitals and indigent relief organizations in the world we had almost forgotten. Just as we had once found a cow groaning in agony, unable to deliver her dead calf, and had performed with a pocket knife a bovine episiotomy, so now we took over this little bit of human flotsam from Baker's dump and nursed him back to health. He was just a bindlestiff, he had no home and he gave us no name. We called him Binney for the "binney" that he wore upon his back.

Binney adopted us. When I opened our dugout door to toss out the morning wash-water, Binney was always sitting there waiting to be asked in to breakfast. At noon he was there for lunch. And come sundown, Binney went up the highway to meet Bill and lead home the burros, like a faithful little dog waiting for a bit of food and a kind word from its adored master. For Binney, the sun rose and set with Bill's coming and going.

But in our little dugout there was no place for Binney to sit while he ate, save on our bunk, and this made me wince. At night after he had gone to his bed in the straw, I carefully took off the top blanket and laid it aside for his exclusive use. I felt sorry for Binney, I told Bill, but I did long for his departure from our crowded midst. Bill was shocked—and Binney stayed.

One evening they came in as usual and immediately behind them stalked a large determined tourist lady and her meek little husband. She poked her head into the stairway and shouted gaily, "May I come in?"

"Why certainly," I replied, dishing up red beans and cutting corn bread into great steaming squares, "Come on down."

"Come on, Herbie," she commanded, and obediently Herbie came.

They perched themselves on our bunk while I wondered what this was all about. "Tell me," she commanded, "what does *he* do with those burros? Why does he wear that beard? How do you make a living? Why do you live in this place—and what is that heavenly food you are cooking?"

"One thing at a time," I smiled. "Why don't you eat with us and let Bill tell you the story?"

"Herbie," she squealed delightedly, "we are invited to dinner," and she edged herself over until she was at the hinged shelf that served as our table.

After supper Binney slipped unobtrusively away and again the lady demanded, "Who is *he*? Tell me about him." We told her the story of Binney and his pneumonia. We told her of our Death Valley days, of our trip across the Strip, of the Mazatals and our return, of the tintype business that Bill had fallen into through no will of his own. She sat speechless, bugeyed, as the hours slipped away. At last we were through, and she straightened up with determination. "You must write!" she declared. "I won't take no for an answer."

In vain I protested that I knew nothing of writing—that no one could just say "Write" and wring powerful phrases from an unwilling scribe. She was, in short, I assured her, barking up the wrong tree when she picked me for a writer.

"I'll send you books," she answered serenely, "and paper, pencils, everything you need."

I shuddered. Was my placid life in Baker going to be upset by this determined lady and her correspondence course?

No sooner had she reached Los Angeles than my correspondence swelled. There came books on "How to Write a Short Story," "Narrative Writing," "Expository Technique" and a dozen more that I never opened. There came a ream of clean white paper, pencils, eraser and even books on "How to Win a Contest." Since I never heard soap operas, this wasn't going to prove much help. There came daily letters, exhorting me to *write, write, write*—write letters, write words, write *anything* just to get in the swing of it!

Somewhere I had read that Zane Grey did his writing of Western stories far removed from the scene, perhaps while on a cruise of the South Seas. I could see why. When one is engaged in *doing* something, it seems of interest only to himself. Maybe some day when I grew old and tired I would feel differently about this writing, but just now I was definitely not interested.

The days slipped by and it was Christmas. My mind went back over the Christmases we had known. There was one in Death Valley when we found a forgotten can of spinach to supplement a wild duck from the salt marshes. And another in the Mazatals when our distant neighbors had sent a dozen eggs and a forequarter of young beef. What would this Christmas bring? Sighing, I studied the leaden skies. If it didn't clear up soon so Bill could get back to work, it seemed that more beans was our prospect.

Christmas morning dawned bright and chill. Bill went up to the highway and came running back. "Got a big package in on the freight van," he puffed. "Got to borrow a wheelbarrow to get it home." What could it be? Once my mother had sent a quart of her famous chow-chow and another of wild strawberry preserves, and the postage had been ninety-six cents. I hoped she hadn't sent her year's canning to me. Bill came trundling the borrowed wheelbarrow, an enormous brown carton on top.

It was from Los Angeles—our gay, firm tourist and her dear

CHRISTMAS COMES TO BINNEY

Herbie ran a sanitarium there. In that package was the most complete and perfect Christmas dinner ever assembled. A roasted chicken, a jar of rich gravy, celery, nuts, cranberry sauce, even potatoes—white and sweet; a mince pie and thick creamy home-made fudge. There were also pajamas for me, socks for Bill and warm messages of cheer from the lady, Herbie, all the sanitarium employees and patients. What a wealth of fun that sanitarium must have had planning our Christmas as the owner trotted from room to room, repeating over and over the story we had told her of our travels.

For us, it was a wonderful heart-warming thing to know that somewhere our adventures had so stirred the imagination of dozens of perfect strangers that they had made this spontaneous gesture of friendliness and good will at Christmas time.

And Binney was not forgotten. There was one package marked "For Binney." We called him in and put it in his thin little outstretched arms. It made us gulp to see him standing there, looking down at his burden with that heart-breaking slow look of wonder, disbelief and incredulous happiness. "For me?" he repeated with a toothless grin, "A Christmas present for *me*?"

"Open it," we urged.

Slowly as if prolonging the ecstasy of anticipation, Binney undid his bundle. He took out a warm gray wool sweater, then a pair of dark gray pants, a gray felt hat, good black shoes, socks, tie and even a handkerchief. There was nothing missing from Binney's new wardrobe. His eyes caressed the warm soft clean clothes—new clothes! He could not speak. Suddenly he gathered up the whole works and ran outdoors. In a few moments he was back, dressed in all his finery. "How do I look?" he chirped, preening himself, arms outstretched like little wings ready for flight. "How do I look in good clothes?"

"You look fine, Binney," we assured him, but Binney did not hear. He had thrust one hand into his new sweater pocket and come out with a crisp one dollar bill. He caressed it, studied it, smoothed out imaginary creases—dreaming—of what? Suddenly Binney straightened up, threw out his chest—and right there, from a crisp new dollar bill and twenty dollars worth of clothes, a new Binney was born.

The next day he left Baker. "Going to hock his new clothes for wine," sneered someone. Not Binney. In a month he was back and Binney was in business. The dollar bill had been invested in needles, pins and razor blades which he was selling from door to door, far from dime store competition. He was gone again and for a time there came no word. Then one day an old car stopped by Bill's stand, and out hopped Binney—possessor of a partner and a car. Binney, a salesman of dignity, was a man of affairs. Binney even had a name and a set of bright new teeth. The bindlestiff was no more.

So it was that this became our most memorable Christmas of all, the Christmas when the kindliness and Christmas spirit of an entire sanitarium staff and patients reached out to the refuse dump of humanity, to lift back to his place in the world a forgotten little bindlestiff.

WE MOVE ON TO ADVENTURE

Tents, leaky cabins, brush wickiups, all paled before the toughening experience of living in a desert dugout. On bright days I left its dark confines to wander out into the clean desert sands, there to sit idly watching the ever-changing pattern of light and shadow on naked brown hills, or the small busy insect life at my feet. After two years of steady hiking, it was good to sit, relaxed, letting the peace and stillness of the desert flow through me.

On days that furious winds came howling down through the draw in which Baker lay, hurling savage blasts of stinging sand, there was no choice but to sit in the tiny cubicle, although the inside of a cement mixer would have done just as well. Wind and sand funneled in through the single opening and finding no exit, swirled and beat around us, filling our eyes, our hair, even our teeth, with the horrible gritty stuff. Bill wondered if human beings were subject to that ailment of burros in which the animal's stom-

225

ach is clogged with settled sand and dirt. If so, our days were certainly numbered. "Adobe stomach" the prospectors called it.

After the winds had passed, we came out blinking, into a world swept clean; clean of rubbish that desert dwellers are prone to toss out their doors, clean of little woodpiles carefully gathered, clean of tin and plywood saved to repair battered shacks. Once a cabin roof sailed away, never to be seen again.

If windy days kept Bill at home, cold or clouds did not. We lived only from one picture to the next and often Bill went to work without a penny. After he had a customer or two I would go up and collect the money to buy our dinner. It was a hand-to-mouth existence but Bill thought it was wonderful that every day the manna fell.

"All we need is fifty cents a day," he declared. "Anything more than that is velvet."

Starting with no knowledge of sales psychology, Bill rapidly learned that his best customers were men and women past forty, preferably those who stopped for a cocktail or a glass of beer. Older people were eager for fun, uninhibited, with more money to spend. Young couples were the poorest hazard, and children Bill discouraged with finality. For one thing, Balboa hated children. We had tamed him after a fashion but he had those rolling red-rimmed eyes, indicative of a mean disposition, and no observant child was ever fooled into trusting him. The only way Bill could work him at all was to keep him exercised into a state of sleepy oblivion by frequent furious gallops across the desert.

On these occasions I was called to tend the camera. One day as I stood waiting for Bill and Balboa to return, a car stopped and a man called out, "Well, well, how's mugging?" I didn't know what mugging was so I stammered for time. The next question was no better. "Playing still all winter?"

While I was still figuring that one, Bill, scenting a possible customer, came in at a dead run, and to my relief took over the conversation. Later I asked, "Bill, what is 'mugging' and what did he mean by 'playing still'?"

"Mugging is taking photos, a mugger is a photographer, and playing still is staying in one place as opposed to going on the road," explained Bill. "That was an old carnie running a three-for-a-dime photo machine. He just made Frontier Days in Barstow and is on his way to Las Vegas to make the Helldorado."

"How did *you* know what he meant, I'd like to know," I persisted.

"I learned the lingo once in a circus when I was water boy for the elephants."

Pretty soon Bill said wistfully, "Edna, why don't we go on the road and make fairs, rodeos and Wild West celebrations?"

You guessed it. We went to Las Vegas to make the rip-snorting annual celebration known as Helldorado. It took ten days to hike it. We made camp on a little creek that ran past the rodeo grounds and once more I was in a strange new world—a world of muggers, spielers, pitchmen—a world in which a woman was an "old hay bag" or simply, an "old bag." Only the lean, hard rodeo hands seemed familiar, in their skin-tight Levis slung perilously low on narrow hips, shirt-tails forever escaping bounds.

For a small fee Bill secured a business license and set up his camera at the curb before the busy Nevada Bar. This bar, immediately off the main street, fronted on a short street that ran through the red-light district known as "the line" or Block Sixteen. Now that Bill needed me to help handle the crowds, I had to get over my shyness and go uptown each day to join him, and my shortest route lay by way of this little street of ill fame. Like all women, I was curious about the girls of the red-light district and I looked out of the corners of my eyes at the green curtains, from behind which peered the faces of watchful women.

Sometimes clad in thin negligees, the girls came out and sat on the sidewalk under the rickety frame awning of the old Honolulu Club. I had to almost trip over their dainty slippers to get by. For years I had not been accustomed to passing people without speaking, so I raised my eyes and said, "Good morning." At first the girls stared woodenly right through me, but I persisted in speaking each time I passed, until at last they greeted me as I approached with a warm "Hello—how's business?"

Now that I had conquered the white girls, I had an irresistible desire to make the yellow woman speak also. On the opposite side of the street, she sat day after day in exactly the same position, on the straight wooden chair, between the sidewalk and the cubicles that housed her colored "girls." Her eyes stared straight before her, she seemed to see nothing, not even the white girls who sometimes called tauntingly to her from their own side of the street. They dared not cross, nor did she, for that was a law laid down, we had heard, after a brawl in the streets over a customer claimed by both sides.

I passed by on the sidewalk and looked the yellow woman straight in the eye. She said nothing. I said, "Good morning." She made no answer. I said it again, a little louder and she grunted a surly "Ugh." I went on puzzled. Where had I seen that staring look before, those dilated unseeing pupils? Ah, I had it! They were the eyes of the cocaine addicts of my Cook County hospital days. No wonder she was able to sit all day immobile as a statue.

Uptown, things were humming. In alley ways and in the recesses of vacant store fronts stood the muggers with their three-for-a-dime machines and pitchmen, pitching everything from gold wire jewelry, silk handkerchiefs, and little celluloid birds fluttering from the end of a stick, to horoscopes and indecent postcards.

When Las Vegas put on this annual celebration designed to recapture the ways of the Old West, she had only to leave well enough alone. Men grew whiskers and wore their loudest plaid shirts, and women appeared on the streets clad in long calico dresses and sunbonnets. Otherwise, except for the crowds, it looked little different from the day we had led the skittering burros down its main street two years before.

Every day of the Helldorado there was a parade, but no spectators. Every man, woman and child was in it, on horseback, in wagons, buckboards, with burros or afoot. I was amused to see one famous Western movie star (Tex Ritter), imported for the occasion, riding his famous horse at the head of the procession and ever crowd-conscious, bowing and smiling to a long expanse of empty sidewalk.

In the bars men stood twelve deep. At the Nevada Bar tourists mingled, unknowingly, with the girls I had seen on the sidewalks, and miners in from the hills. The girls were Bill's best customers. They dragged out aging admirers and egged them into a dozen pictures apiece, gaily tossing to Bill part of the money that was free and easy stuff during the hectic days of Helldorado.

One day there was a stir and commotion in the bar, and someone came out, waving in the crowd. "Everybody inside for free drinks," he yelled, "and bring the jackass there," indicating the skittish Balboa hastily backing away from the scene of confusion. Willing hands grabbed his halter and Balboa was dragged, sitting flatly on his rump, across the sidewalk into the saloon and behind the bar, where they tied a white apron around his neck and ordered the bartender across the bar to join the fun.

The occasion for the party, said someone near us, was a wedding—a wedding to be performed right here in a few moments. The justice of the peace was waiting, a little the worse for the wait, and happily at ease with a crowd of girls from the "block." The bride was also one of the girls, marrying her "business manager," her polite name for the lowest profession of man. After the ceremony, she threw her arms around his neck and whispered happily, "Honey, I'll make you a *million* dollars!" Looking critically at her hennaed hair and early crow's feet, I murmured under my breath, "Honey, you'll have to step on it. Time's a-wastin'!"

After the show was over and the spielers, pitchmen and muggers were gone, it was like old times in our camp by the creek. Drawn by the warmth of our campfire, strangers who passed by night stopped to visit, and there was hardly an evening that saw us alone.

One night a cowhand appeared with a tiny coyote pup from a litter he had dug out of their den in some rocks. It was so tiny that its eyes were still blue, its coat just rough wool, and its tail as clean as a rat's. Mocking the call of a coyote, Bill threw back his head and let out a long low wail, ending on a mournful crescendo. Instantly, the baby coyote sat down, threw back his little head, opened up his throat and emitted an exact copy of Bill's coyote call. Bill was charmed and begged the man to sell him the pup. After that other one left on the Death Valley roadside, we named him Ishawipe, the Shoshone word for coyote. As before, we soon shortened it to Ishy.

Bill was still sold on making Western shows. I wondered how we were to navigate from Las Vegas to Cheyenne and on to Pendleton on foot before the season was over, to say nothing of how we were to find living quarters in these cities with two burros, a dog and a coyote to care for. But as usual, I left it up to Bill. I would continue to tag along wherever he led.

Little did I know that in only six short weeks we would be camped scarcely a cannon shot from the towering skyline of New York.

Burro Bill and Balboa waiting to photograph
tourists in front of Failing's Cafe, Baker, California.

WE MEET A DUDE

I was standing over the fire stirring up the beans when I saw Bill coming down the creekbank with a young man in tow. I reached into the kyacks, fished out another tin cup and plate, hit them on the edge of the kyack to shake out the sand, and by the time I was ready Bill was saying, "This is Bob—he's from New Jersey."

It wasn't necessary to tell me that he came from back East, for he was as bareheaded as the day he was born, and in Las Vegas a man would no more appear on the streets without a hat than he would without his pants.

While Bob was sitting gingerly on an empty pack-box struggling vainly with pants creases, beans, coffee and flies all at once, I looked him over. He had one of those bland smooth faces with no bones showing through, and unrevealing short-sighted eyes behind expensive tinted glasses. He didn't look nearly so interesting as our friends like Speedy, Ozark Jim, or even Baggy Britches. When he left I thought I had seen the last of him; but no, he was back for dinner, bringing a carton of ice cream. Seating himself on the pack-box again, he waited for his plate.

After that Bob showed up for lunch and dinner every day, soon changing from his dark business suit to a gaudy pink and blue plaid shirt and stiff new Levis that seemed so awkward when worn hitched up to the normal waist line. Levis belong at half mast as every cowhand knows, and a Stetson needs wearing to develop its personality. Bob's was just a hard new hat circled by a beaded hat-band. But Bob was confident that no one now could suspect his recent arrival from the shores of Jersey.

Everything Western intrigued him, and one day he said to Bill, "It seems that everyone out here has a nickname. There's Diamondfield Jack, Death Valley Scotty, Seldom Seen Slim, and you are Burro Bill. I'd like a nickname, too. What do you think would be good?"

"How about Alkali Ike?" we suggested, but Bob shook his head.

"No, I think I'll be Malachite Bob," he answered.

"Why Malachite?"

"Well, I haven't told you much about myself, but I'm in the dye business in New Jersey, and I discovered a color process that has made me independent. The color that gave me my start was called 'malachite green'. It's the green you see on every can of Del Monte brand canned goods. For sentimental reasons, I'd like to use that for a name."

Malachite he was from that day on. But what pleasure he got from sitting around our camp, I couldn't understand. There were so many interesting things a man could if he had money, why did he just sit? We tried to interest him in a boat trip down the

WE MEET A DUDE

Colorado River or a pack trip through the Grand Canyon country to the Havasupai Reservation, but no.

What Malachite wanted, he finally admitted, was to take a prospecting trip with us.

"But you say you have to leave in three weeks," protested Bill. "We could hardly get out of Las Vegas in that length of time. There would be no time left to prospect."

"Then we'll buy a truck," said Malachite calmly, "and take the outfit as far as we wish and then get out and hike."

As casually as we might buy a pound of beans, he purchased the truck and put it in Bill's name, and the two of them began rebuilding it for the trip. The truck bed was divided by a slatted partition—one half for the burros, the other for Bill and me, with a built-in bunk. Over it they stretched a canvas roof with an air-space under the eaves, to Bill's bitter disappointment. He wanted a prairie schooner but Malachite thought that was carrying Western atmosphere a little too far.

When it was done, we loaded the burros and their packs, our little tent for Malachite, put the dog and coyote on our bunk, and were off.

For the next two weeks we roamed the desert, searching, it developed, for a tungsten mine since that was an ore needed by Malachite in his dye industry. He had a handbook for prospectors, glass test tubes, vials of acids and other things that made prospecting a far cry from the days when a man needed only a small egg-frying pan and a bit of water to do his sampling.

We didn't find any tungsten, but Malachite didn't care. He was happily collecting cactus plants, rusty relics, purple bottles and ore specimens, exactly as we had done during our first year on

235

the desert. His chief treasure was a desert chuckawalla, one of those vegetarian lizards that look like miniature dinosaurs straight from the Field Museum.

When Balboa saw a herd of wild burros and ran off to join them, Malachite seized the opportunity to drive back to Vegas and hire a cowboy and horse to come and rope the erring burro back into the fold. It was his chance for some good color movies and we dressed the horse in the brightest saddle blanket that Malachite could find.

"Think your horse can catch a wild jackass?" Bill inquired skeptically.

"Sure," bragged the cowpoke, "This ol' boy can outrun anything on four legs."

For two days Ol' Boy and rider charged and re-charged, striving desperately to herd Balboa into a box canyon and toss a rope around his neck. Balboa kept in the open, snorting defiance, and ran circles around Ol' Boy, always returning to a certain lank old jenny of his choice. This jenny had a beautiful fuzzy little black colt about six weeks old, and at last we settled with the cowboy for her, in lieu of Balboa. We tied her at the water hole, her mother came to her and Balboa came to his jenny. Bill drove the truck across the trail and as suddenly as he had left us, Balboa walked up to Bill and meekly put his nose in the halter. His romantic interlude was over.

The colt we called Chiquita. She never seemed to know the difference between me and the rawboned old jenny that bore her. She flopped in my lap, followed my every footstep, and slept by my side. I fed her at first, by punching two holes in a can of milk, and

236

later taught her to drink from the shallow gold-pan that served as a feed-pan for the burros and a wash basin for us. Chiquita not only drank canned milk, but she also guzzled up all of our warm soapy wash water, so that we never again got to use it over and over as was our custom in dry camps.

When I started cooking at night there was Chiquita nuzzling at my elbow, begging for her milk, Ishawipe the coyote, wagging his whole woolly little body and whining for his can of dog food, Slats wriggling and showing her teeth in an ingratiating grin as she reminded me that she was hungry also. Off to one side, Balboa and Jack would be onking pitifully, their big eyes following every move of the multi-purpose gold-pan—and sitting over the fire would be Bill and Malachite, hungrily lifting lids and poking into pots. I felt just like the old woman who lived in a shoe.

Sometimes Chiquita reminded me of that wistful goat Mariole, in her embarrassing devotion. After we returned to Las Vegas, she followed me to the stores and stood outside onking softly through plate glass windows, to the consternation of shopkeepers. Once I went into a public restroom and left Chiquita outside. Suddenly a terrific shriek rent the air, the compartment next to me flew open and out dashed an irate and disheveled woman. As the half-door banged shut behind her, from under it crawled a thoroughly abashed little black burro. I pretended I didn't know her, but she ran straight to me and hid behind my back, peeking timidly at the woman who screamed, "Is that *your* animal? I'll have you arrested! Bringing *bears* into public places!" I walked meekly away, Chiquita running along bumping her head against my legs.

Las Vegas, I told Bill, was too congested for us and our animals. How soon could we ship Malachite's treasures to New Jersey and be on our way to the next show? We put it up to Malachite and he considered.

"How," he asked abruptly, "would you folks like to see New York?"

"I don't want to see it bad enough to walk a year to get there," was Bill's reply.

"No, really," protested Malachite. "You'd be a sensation in New York. People would go nuts over your burros, and those pictures you take. Tell you what, you take the truck and haul my collection back for me, and I'll pay all expenses. Take your outfit and camera—why, you'll make a fortune, man. Just go as you are—long hair, beard and all, and don't get a new hat. That old one is perfect, sweat stains and all."

Bill and I had heard plenty about New York from visiting rodeo hands and we had no illusions about making a fortune. But more than anything in the world I wanted to see my family again, so I persuaded Bill that Virginia and New Jersey were pretty close together—that is, they bordered on the same ocean, and perhaps after we were back there we could figure out some way to get me to Virginia.

Had I foreseen the "sensation" that we were to create in the East, I would have gone as fast as my legs would take me— straight back across the Arizona Strip.

WEST MEETS EAST

For several days Bill and Malachite kept me on the run to and from the village, fetching endless nuts, bolts, grommets and related bits of hardware that vanished into the body of the big truck as they remodeled it for our eastbound trip. At last they threw down their tools and stood back, beaming in satisfaction.

"Come and see how you like your new home," called Malachite.

He seemed so pleased that I restrained the shudder I felt creeping up my spine as I beheld the unwieldly monstrosity, the dry-land ark that was to bear me back to my girlhood home. After an absence of nearly ten years, I was going home—in this!

From the corners of the canvas roof, purple bottles swung crazily. On the cab door of the driver's side was fastened Bill's rawhide rifle scabbard, the one he had made himself from an old dry cowhide soaked to pliability in a pond of drinking water on the Arizona Strip. Over the cab was nailed his favorite emblem, a crossed pick and shovel, above a large miner's gold-pan. None of these did I mind, nor yet the fact that the burros' boudoir was separated from ours by only a few slats. I didn't really mind that each night we must shove Chiquita out of our bedroom and swab the deck before we ourselves could move in; nor that the coyote, Ishy, and the dog, Slats, were to occupy our bed by day; nor that our privacy would be nil, due to the wide air-space under the canvas roof: no, none of these did I mind. What had *me* worried were the two mammoth bleached white cow-skulls, grinning cosily above our heads. How could I gather up sufficient aplomb to ride down the long leafy aisle of dignified old Duke of Gloucester Street in Williamsburg, past the houses of genteel Virginians who were my mother's neighbors, beneath the leering faces of those infernal long-dead cows?

I was a little comforted by the fact that no one paid much attention to us as we rode through Las Vegas to take Malachite to his plane. But then, in Las Vegas even Lady Godiva would have caused scarcely a ripple.

We pulled back on the highway and headed for Utah.

Utah and Wyoming were fine—wide open spaces, good places to camp and graze the burros, and as for curiosity, there was only an occasional query, "Headin' for the Roundup at Cheyenne?" So Nebraska came as a shock. All day we had driven on Nebraska's built-up roadways, finding no place to pull off the road to make camp or even to unload the burros for a rest from their tortured squatting position. At nightfall we were growing desperate when Bill suddenly exclaimed, "I know! The stockyards! That's what the rodeo hands do when they go East. They unload at the stock-yards."

At the next town we turned toward the railroad tracks and sure enough, near the depot was a small fenced stockpen and loading platform, a big shade tree and a spigot of water—as fine a camp as anyone could ask. It had not been used for a long time and green grass grew in the fenced enclosures. Bill unloaded the tired burros and watched them roll like cats in a bed of catnip while I started a pot of spaghetti.

Pretty soon a farmer and his wife stopped to gaze, then another one or two, and by the time I had propped up the tailgate of the truck and spread it with a clean canvas and our cups and plates, there were at least one hundred bystanders interestedly watching our every move. Bill called cheerily, "Good evening, folks," but got no response. I pumped up the little gasoline campstove we had bought in Las Vegas and finished my cooking. Nobody left, so I resigned myself to eating before one hundred spectators, and we sat down. One woman, bolder than the rest, came forward then and peered into the spaghetti pot. "What do you eat?" she asked curiously, and seeing the contents, she called to the others with obvious disappointment, "They eat just like we do—it's spaghetti."

Dark came on and still the crowd hung around, silent, watchful, waiting for something to happen. I filled the gold-pan with warm water and washed my face. So did Bill. I brushed my teeth. So did Bill. Fascinated, two hundred eyes followed our every motion.

Chiquita romped in for her soapy wash-water and followed it up with three cans of milk. Ishy, having finished his eager exploring, was busily chewing up the remains of a putrescent dead crow, meanwhile keeping a wary eye on Slats who only looked disdainfully the other way. We fed them both, tied them to the truck wheels, and Chiquita at the door to our compartment to keep her from honking her loneliness to the stars, and we were ready for bed. Still the watchful eyes stared out in the darkness that surrounded our camp.

Bill turned out the gasoline lantern, we climbed the short ladder to our bunk, and went to bed. As we drifted to sleep we heard out of the darkness, "Ain't that the damnedest beard you ever see? Must be they come from the House of David."

On through Iowa and into Illinois, the farther east we traveled, the thicker grew the crowds that watched our nightly ablutions. It was in Joliet that we brushed our teeth in plain view of no less than five hundred spectators. As we drove into Joliet, Balboa somehow caught a rear leg in the slats of the partition and lamed himself. Bill's first concern was ever for the welfare of his burros, so we stopped at the first opening we came to, a vacant lot across from a cheap saloon in the colored section of town—and there we camped. The colored kids came on the run and made a wonderful new game of scrambling into our truck by means of the ladder, then over the slats to the burros' compartment, down the cleated tailgate and up the ladder again.

There were so many of them, Bill and I sat helpless, unable to cook or in fact to do anything but watch out for our animals as best we could. I wanted to move on, but Bill shook his head stubbornly. "I'm going to keep that burro on the ground till his leg is well, if we have to stay here a week."

Just then the saloon doors swung out to emit a staggering citizen, bent on stopping the children's noise. "Hey you kids," he began and stopped. His eyes grew wild with terror as he turned and hurtled back through the swinging doors, screaming, "Help! There's a *bear* loose!" Poor little Chiquita again!

WEST MEETS EAST

After the children had been called home to bed, their parents began drifting in, and soon the vacant lot was solidly packed. There was nothing silent about these visitors—they asked questions and chattered and visited among themselves, having a most delightful get-together long after we had turned out our lights and gone to bed. Ishy seemed to excite their curiosity, for none of them had seen a coyote, nor ever heard of one. To them he was a strange "wild dog" and they kept a respectful distance from his eager exploring nose.

The next morning Balboa had scarcely a limp, so we left the dreary grimy vacant lot. Soon we stopped on the main street of a large town to buy groceries. A man rushed out from his clothing store and demanded excitedly, "What you selling? What you got? I buy some." On being assured that we had nothing to sell, he looked so disappointed that Bill offered him a piece of Malachite's blue copper ore, which he seized with delight although he still wanted to buy the plaid shirts off our backs "for a souvenir." Crowds began to gather again and seeing the blue ore, began to clamor for their free samples, too. Fearful of leaving Malachite with no trophies of his Western trip, Bill hurriedly backed out and yelled, "Adios, amigos" as he drove away. "Some kind of a furriner," somebody remarked resignedly.

In Ohio, the hedges along the roadside were hanging with vines upon which grew huge shining dewberries. Remembering that out West the state highway claims sixty feet on each side of the road, we calculated by eye that these berries were well within the highway boundaries and as such, free to any traveler who chose to pick them. We pounced on them and began eating when suddenly a bullet swished through the air followed by a loud

243

report, and a harsh voice from a house nearby, "Leave them berries be!" We were so astonished we could scarcely climb back into the truck, but at last I remembered that "back East" the farmers claim all, regardless of where the fruit falls.

In Pennsylvania we no longer needed to hunt for stockyards at night. Here were beautiful pine-clad hills, streams, springs, and here, we discovered, grew more game than in any other state of the Union. Here, also, was the most degrading, the bitterest poverty we had ever seen, in the tumbledown shacks of the coal miners, perched at the very entrances of the mines, amid incredible filth and grime. The women's washings hung limply, gray, dispirited damp garments, in the smoke and fog that never lifted from the face of the shining sun. We thought of the boundless sunshine, the clean sands of the West, and wondered if these people realized to what a dismal life sentence they had been committed. All through our lives, the name of this town would spell man's misery at its lowest ebb.

One day we stopped for lunch at a lovely woodland spot. An old man was tramping leisurely along the road, a long stick over his shoulder on the end of which he carried his worldly goods tied up in a red bandana. We opened our bedroom door and Chiquita leaped to the ground as gracefully as a mountain goat. The old man stopped. He regarded Chiquita with wonder, incredulity and delight. He dropped his stick and ran to put his arms around her neck, falling to his knees in the soft grass. "Ah-hh-h," he crooned into her velvety long ears, "At last! All my life I've heard about ye. Me old mither told me about ye, and now I've seen ye. Ye're the little darlin'—the little one that gives milk for the sick wee ones— ye're the little nanny goat. God bless ye!"

WEST MEETS EAST

Once by the roadside we saw a spring of clear water. In the West there would have been a sign for the traveler, "WATER AHEAD," but here there was nothing. We stopped and took out our lunch. A car drove up with several occupants, a nice car and well-spoken people. "Do you know that you are trespassing?" asked one man pleasantly. Bill looked wonderingly at the open spot only a few feet from the highway, at the spring of water, unfenced, and said honestly, "No sir, I did not. Out where we live this would be state property, open to all travelers."

"Where are you from?—Oh, I see—NeVAHda. Now just where is NeVAHda, anyhow?"

Bill began bounding Nevada, on the west by California, on the east by Utah, etc., when the woman interrupted, "I went to California once. Did I go near Nevada?"

"Where did you go in California?" asked Bill.

"To San Francisco."

"Do you remember Reno, the 'Biggest Little City in the World'?" Bill asked.

"Why certainly, that's where people get quick divorces."

"Well, you passed right through Reno," said Bill, "and Reno is the biggest city in Nevada."

"Why, yes!" she screamed triumphantly, turning to the others, "I've been in Nevada!"

"That," remarked Bill, as we drove away, "reminds me of the American tourist in Europe who admonished his guide, 'Never mind the towns—just call out the *countries* we go through.'"

Edna and William Price, San Francisco, California. Early 1930s.

CAMP IN A COURTYARD

In the red brick factory district of Paterson, New Jersey, a summer twilight was settling down in a haze of smoke and grime, over dingy streets, over buildings standing elbow to elbow with faces sadly in need of a wash. From Nevada to New Jersey, for twenty-one nights, we had found camps where the animals could rest on soft earth and stretch and roll to their heart's content, and where we ourselves could cook and sleep in the open. Now, at the end of the road, we were met with dismal sidewalks and factory walls, no spot unpaved or untrod.

We stopped at a booth and phoned Malachite. "Come right to the factory," he commanded, "I have all arrangements made."

A staring policeman directed us to the block on Market Street that housed a number of small factories, among them Malachite's dye works. There was an archway leading into a dingy cinder-strewn courtyard, deserted now that the workers had left for the night. Malachite stepped out of the shadows, beaming with relief. "Thought you'd never get here," he observed. "Only took me fifteen hours to fly back and you've been three weeks. Wouldn't that old truck do any better than that?"

"We weren't running a marathon," grunted Bill. "We were watching the scenery—not the speedometer. Where do we camp tonight?"

"Right here," replied Malachite. "I've told all the workers in all the buildings on this block about you, and showed them our color movie, and they are all waiting to see you camp, and cook, and ride Balboa—I told them how he bucks, and you've got to show them how."

I glanced at Bill out of the corner of my eye and saw the consternation on his face that I felt upon my own. "In this place? Why, Balboa will get so filthy rolling in those sooty cinders he'll need another bath and bluing rinse before we can take a single picture. You know I keep him spotless, and where in Paterson can you bathe a burro? And besides, with all these people coming and going, I'd feel like a damned fool sitting here by a campfire cooking beans. Let's drive out in the country and camp."

"No," said Malachite firmly, "I will not disappoint all these people. Why, man, that's all they've talked about for weeks! They know all about the burros, the coyote, and you, and they've followed your trip every step of the way. You have no idea what a break this is in the monotony of their lives, Bill."

That did it, of course. Bill, the freedom-loving, the adventurous, was the last to deny anyone a bit of color or romance in a drab existence.

Refusing to leave his animals unattended, Bill left them on the truck and, adding Malachite to our entourage, we drove out to dinner. Malachite pointed out a large well-lit cafe and, parking the truck in front, we went in and sat down. Our order was taken by a goggle-eyed waiter who stared fixedly at Bill's ears.

I had forgotten Bill's ears were a novelty. Once, in an impulsive moment, he had pierced his earlobes and hung them with a pair of silver and turquoise earrings purchased from an Indian. Pleased with the effect, Bill continued to wear them and after a year or two I had grown used to them, as I had to his bushy red beard and flowing hair. I rarely noticed anymore their electrifying effect on strangers. Fascinated, the waiter backed away, looking as though he expected something even more surprising than turquoise earrings to pop out of Bill's thick red beard.

By the time our food arrived there were people who had read our license plates, standing around our table, bending over our plates, staring into our faces, feeling of our clothing, and demanding, "Tell us about Nevada."

Bill seemed to be enjoying himself. He settled back in his chair and began a nostalgic paean of praise.

"Nevada?" he murmured, "Why, it's just like all the West— where no man fences his neighbors out, nor himself in. It's a land of deserts and bare hills, of skies and stars—millions of stars— and the moon is so bright you can see to pick up a pin. You can walk for days and never meet a soul. It's—OUCH!"

Over his face shot a look of pain as a woman's scream rose in triumph. "I got one! I got one of his hairs!"

Then pandemonium broke. Seized by a strange mob hysteria, women pounced and tore at Bill's hair and beard, and even tried to tear bits from his woolen shirt. Terrified, shirt-tail flying, he made a dash for the door, Malachite and I hard on his heels. The proprietor was there to hurry us on. "Take them away," he implored. "Never mind the bill—just take the people away or they will break up my place."

There was another crowd at the front, noses pressed to the glass window. We ducked and ran, reaching the truck with half a dozen people clinging to the sides as we drove off. Bill turned. "Watch out for the coyote!" he yelled, "He'll bite!" Hurriedly, they dropped off and we drove back to the sheltering walls of the factory yard. Innocently Ishy jumped into my lap and started through my pockets with his inquisitive little nose, for the candy that I always carried for him. He had never bitten anyone in his short little life.

"Whew," observed Bill, "that's what the rodeo hands meant when they told us about these wild Easterners. I'd rather meet a herd of wild steers any day."

The next morning the workers entered the factory by the front but about 9 a.m. someone threw open a window and discovered our arrival. In a flash every window was flung wide, and from each one hung dozens of people, waving, yelling, asking to see the animals. "Ride the black and white one," they demanded. "Let's see him buck. We want to see you cook. Where's the camp-fire?"

Obligingly Bill saddled Balboa and, jumping on his back, rode him around and around the court, Balboa bucking furiously each time he felt Bill's sharp heels dig into his flanks. The janitor arrived with little blocks of wood, tiny ends of lumber, for our fire. I was used to baking with all kinds of fuel, even dried cowchips from the plains of Nevada, but these seemed fairly hopeless. There is no heat in charred bits of lumber. However, I managed some pretty fair biscuits and a pan of jerky gravy with the aid of

250

the gasoline campstove, another curiosity to the people of the pavements. Since the workers continued to hang from the windows, and not a hand had been turned by 10 o'clock, the managers called a holiday and sent for us to visit the plants.

This proved to be a most enjoyable experience. The workers, faced in their own environment, were suddenly shy and quiet, eager to show us every detail of their work as we had shown them ours. First was the plant that made fifty-cent neckties for such stores as J.C. Penney's. The girls showed us heavy rayons of Roman stripes and asked what kind of ties we wore. "Just triangular neckerchiefs," I answered. So they cut some large gay triangles of material and ran them up with a picoted edge for us. In the ribbon factory the girls ran off yards and yards of weighted gold and silver ribbon and handed it to us, saying, "Take this back to the Indians."

The most interesting plant was a lace factory, owned and operated by a family of lace-makers who had learned their trade in England as children. They paid themselves salaries, the highest being thirty-five dollars a week for the man who operated a loom with three thousand threads. The fabric was woven of white and pale flesh tones, to aid in detecting a single broken thread instantly so as to shut off the loom and tie the thread before the continuity of the pattern was interrupted. This operator worked standing, his eyes shuttling back and forth across the three thousand threads so fast it made us dizzy.

The lace weavers gave us so many yards of wide all-over lace that I was later able to curtain much of my mother's big old Virginia home. I knew that in the houses of Mrs. Bill there would never be need for such delicate things as these.

BURRO BILL AND ME

On the following day, Malachite wanted a dinner of beans and jerky gravy for some of his friends. All morning Bill and I wandered through the markets of Paterson searching for our familiar pink beans of the West. All we found were navies, limas and kidney. Malachite insisted they must be pink. They tasted different, he said.

"Well, I can't find them," I said. "You go look."

Malachite called his secretary, a briskly efficient young woman, and thrust a bill into her hands. "Go out," he said, "and don't come back without pink beans."

"*Pink* beans?" she asked as if he had gone daft. "Don't you mean kidney beans?"

"No," roared Malachite, "I mean *pink* beans."

At nightfall there was a call from the secretary. "I've been all over Paterson and Passaic and in between," she wailed. "Won't you settle for kidney beans?"

"No," yelled Malachite. "Go to New York first thing in the morning. Get *pink* beans if you have to fly to Arizona after them."

Late the next afternoon, a weary young woman tramped truculently into Malachite's office and dumped a brown paper sack on his desk. "There," she said tartly, "are your pink beans. I had everyone in New York crazy hunting pink beans for me. I called up the best wholesalers and the best hotels and they offered to fly them back from Arizona, but finally someone sent me to the foreign settlement where a few Mexicans live. Did you know that only Mexicans eat pink beans?"

"And so do we," we chorused, grabbing the bag of little pink pellets. "Let's put them to soak for our banquet in the cinders."

252

CAMP IN A COURTYARD

After the workers had departed for the night, we built up a bonfire, innocently disregarding any ideas the fire department might have. Fortunately, we were well hidden from view or our visit might also have included the Paterson hoosegow.

The visitors were enthusiastic about our pink beans, or frijoles, cooked with salt pork and twelve garlic buttons floating on top, and our light tender sourdough rolls. But for the jerky gravy, a gray gluey mass, they did not seem to share Bill's and Malachite's enthusiasm. Even Bill had to admit that jerky gravy eaten over a scrap lumber fire in a cinder-strewn factory courtyard was not exactly an epicurean delight.

Bill, Edna, Chief Hummingbird with Balboa in 1937.

OF PICTURES
AND POLITICS

Now that the preliminary courtesies were over, Bill was eager to begin work. "Where," he asked Malachite, "do we get a permit to take pictures?"

"My secretary," replied Malachite grandly, "knows the secretary to the mayor of Passaic. We will have you introduced to the mayor and everything will be fixed. You haven't a worry in the world."

The mayor was a big soft man, somewhat coarsened by easy living. We found him apparently facing a boring day, for he grasped our hands eagerly and ushered us into his office. Motioning us to comfortable chairs, he rubbed his pudgy hands together and exclaimed, "Now tell me your story."

"What we want is a permit to take pictures on the streets or in the park," said Bill.

"What kind of pictures? What do you mean?" queried the mayor.

BURRO BILL AND ME

"Come outside and see," replied Bill, and we tripped out to the truckload of animals.

"My idea," explained Bill, "is to set up a miniature desert with the cactus, ore, coyote, chuckawalla and burros saddled for a prospecting trip, and take pictures of people on one burro, leading the other one. Do you think it will go over?"

"Perfect!" exclaimed the mayor delightedly. "It will be a sensation! It's educational—why, we might even get you to take a tour of the schools and talk to the children, and—now let me see, you ought to get at least six hundred pictures out of each school! I'll get in touch with the Board of Education . . ."

"Not so fast," protested Bill. "All I want right now is to make some ready cash. How about just a permit to get on the streets with this outfit?"

"Sure, sure," agreed the mayor. "I'll call the police department and get you a special officer to go with you tomorrow and find a place and stay with you during the day."

"But I don't need the police," Bill persisted. "All I want is a permit."

Then the mayor was struck with a brilliant thought. "Tonight is the rally in the park. We'll have speakers, a movie, radio hookup—and *you* shall be on the program. Think of the advertising value!"

We offered to bring along the color movie of Malachite's invasion of the West.

That night saw us seated on a platform in Passaic's park staring fixedly ahead or at the back of the current speaker. An hour is a long time on a platform. Malachite's movie was received rather woodenly, as though the audience felt no identity with this kind of life. They woke up a little when the cowpoke and Ol' Boy charged after Balboa, and at last they stood up and yelled when he caught Chiquita and dumped her in my lap.

"And now," said the mayor rising gallantly, "is the time to introduce our friends from Nevada—the people who took the wonderful true movie you have just seen. May I present my good friends, Burro Bill and Mrs. Bill from the great West!"

He sat down to a patter of applause, and someone pushed Bill to the microphone. He stepped forward briskly and made a graceful little speech. Then someone grabbed me and shoved me in front of Bill. "Say something, say something," I heard a sibilant whisper behind me.

I grabbed the mouthpiece and stammered, "It is nice to be here—we are having a wonderful time," backed up and sat down with a terrible thud. Why hadn't anyone told me that microphones do not carry your voice decently away into the ether but permit your words to bounce back in your face and scare you out of your wits?

The next morning we were escorted to the same park by a uniformed special officer. We selected a spot and got ready. It was Saturday and kids began to appear from behind every bush. "Take our pictures," they begged.

"Go home and git yer money thin," commanded the Irish cop. One or two scampered off, but most of them hung on the truck or draped themselves over the saddle.

"My maw ain't got no money," said one, teetering on the saddle.

"Mine neither," cried another.

"Then get up and I'll take a free picture for you to take your mother for a present," offered Bill, thinking to eliminate the worst clamberers.

The kids, delighted, ran home with their pictures and were back in minutes, dragging a number of smaller fry. "Mom says take theirs, too," they demanded.

"Git on with ye," ordered the cop.

"Try and make us," taunted the kids, and in a flash the mob was on us, scrambling over the frightened Balboa, hanging upside down from Jack's saddle, poking at the coyote, laughing and screaming epithets at the cop.

Furiously he whipped out his billy and began to beat the knuckles of the clinging little monkeys, forcing them to drop to the ground. Sickened, Bill folded his tripod, picked up his belongings and prepared to leave.

"Leave the kids alone," he said. "It's not their fault. We are just in the wrong place."

Passaic, for a mugger, was definitely out.

THE WILD WEST—
EASTERN STYLE

The next day Bill and I ran away. Away from Malachite, away from the mayor and his shoddy shallow world.

We drove slowly along the beautiful New Jersey boulevards, looking for a place to camp. "This time," declared Bill, "we'll stay away from the cities. We learned our lesson, fooling with politicians in order to save a license fee. We'll find a little summer resort that is unincorporated."

A few hours later found us at Budd Lake, New Jersey. It looked good. There was an arcade for dining and dancing and Bill got the manager's permission to set up his camera, facing the lake shore, hard by the arcade entrance, where no one entering Budd Lake could miss him.

Then we set out to hunt a camp. It isn't easy to find a camp in an Eastern resort where there is no foot of land unoccupied, unfenced or un-posted. In despair, Bill hunted up the chief of police, told him our troubles, and in ten minutes we not only had a camp and a pasture for the animals but we also had a friend in the chief. He took us to his own small farm and there we set up housekeeping by the roadside, while Chiquita, Jack and Balboa kicked up their heels in fourteen acres of soft grass beside the chief's astonished cow.

Each day we drove the truck to our place of business, unloaded and tied the animals, and set out the potted barrel cacti, the boxes of ore, and screened cage with its occupant, the chuckawalla. All this was supposed to put the customer in a desert mood where he would see nothing incongruous in having his picture made on a desert burro.

On the deserts of Arizona, California and Nevada, a tourist was quick to catch on, but now we discovered that when one is going about his daily life, intent on new shoes and the price of potatoes, he cannot be suddenly jerked into an alien world by the mere sight of a potted cactus and a couple of cow-skulls. Bill tried softening his approach by a brief educational spiel.

A man sauntered by and halted. Faced with these unfamiliar animals on a New Jersey shore, he seemed puzzled. "And what," he inquired at last, "are these little animals?"

"Burros," replied Bill, racing into his spiel. "We use them on the Western deserts for saddle animals and for packing in the remote regions."

"And what are you doing with them here?" asked the man.

"Taking pictures," responded Bill. "Hop right on and get your picture made while you wait."

"Oh no, no thank you," the man demurred. "I wouldn't think of taking your time. I suppose you are heading back to the deserts. But I still don't understand—just what do you do for a *living*?"

THE WILD WEST—EASTERN STYLE

To this Bill could find no delicate explanation, so that was a customer lost. Another walked up to the mouse-gray burro, patted him kindly and said, "So this is the little coyote I've heard about." Another, pointing to the coyote, asked, "And is this a little prairie dog from out West?"

But the climax came when a man walked briskly up to Bill and pointed to the largest barrel cactus. "Tell me," he demanded, "do those things or do they not throw their quills?"

"No," said Bill gently, "You are thinking of porcupines. Porcupines do not throw their quills."

"I knew it!" was the triumphant reply. "You can't fool me on anything about the West."

At sunset we drove home, followed by all the women and children on our little road, anxious to know how the day had gone for us. We had been adopted into the hearts of these summer people, seeking respite from the heat of city pavements. They were well-off people, small manufacturers, but they had not traveled, and their ideas of the West were gleaned entirely from the movies.

Every evening they gathered around our campfire to hear of our life in Arizona and Nevada. We couldn't convince them that there were deserts in California—that state to them was only beaches, palms and pretty girls. Nor could they comprehend the distances we had covered. To them, one's life went on in one place—certainly not in three states at once. Our mention of towns like Las Vegas or Flagstaff also puzzled them. "But you said it was desert," they protested. "Now you say there are cities!" Just as some Westerners pictured the East Coast as one solid industrial area like Passaic.

BURRO BILL AND ME

We had felt a little uneasy about deserting Malachite, so we wrote and told him where we were. One evening he dropped in and sat by our fire with our neighbors. He seemed pleased that we had found a place for ourselves and had become independent.

"The mayor is frantic," he grinned. "He phones every day to know what happened to you."

"Don't tell him," we warned. "He'll have us on another round of appearances. We can't live on speeches and news photos and an occasional free lunch. But there's one place we'd like to see before we head West. How about showing us New York?"

WE SEE AND ARE SEEN

New York! Out of a subterranean city we had climbed the stairway leading to the surface world, directly beneath the clock that marked Times Square at Forty-second Street. We were in the heart of a great city, and Malachite's secretary stood back and waited for us to be stricken dumb.

At this time of morning, bright sunshine flooded the street. The scene was exactly as we had pictured it a thousand times, but the wonder, the awe that we had anticipated, was missing. Was it because the human eye was too circumscribed in reach to comprehend its vastness? Or was it because we had lived so long under the great dome of heaven, that all man-made structures seemed dwarfed by comparison? Our first sight of New York was distinctly disappointing.

"Where shall we go first?" asked the girl.

"Macy's!" we answered promptly.

Seeing Macy's was like seeing New York. There was too much of it for any clear impression. The secretary led us to the escalators. "Have you ever ridden an escalator?" she asked.

263

"No, I'd be afraid I'd miss that step-off and fall on my face," I declined. Then glancing behind us I noticed the crowds were closing in. "Let's get on this thing quick!" I urged Bill.

But it was too late. In a moment the crowd had turned and was surging toward the moving staircase, fighting for places. We looked back: the escalator was solid with passengers, standing transfixed, their eyes glued fast on *us!* Hurriedly, we leaped off at the next landing and rushed for the stairs, dragging our guide behind us.

Bill saw the tobacco counter and made a dash for it, looking fearfully behind him. He had barely time to buy a pipe and a package of tobacco when the crowd was again at our heels. We dashed for the street.

"I need some camera supplies," said Bill, as we moved safely away. "Let's hunt up that camera supply house where we order our stuff, and buy some cards and mounts." In a telephone book we found it to be on Delancey Street. It was down under the "el" that we came upon it, a door jammed into the wall. We entered a small room, completely taken up with boxes, camera supplies spewing everywhere, save for a narrow aisle down the center. The proprietor looked at us in amazement.

"You in show business?" he asked in a rapid staccato. "You wear that beard in your business? Earrings, too? Jeez, what some people do to make a living!"

He overturned boxes, rummaged through top layers, and eventually emerged from the disorder, triumphantly clutching the desired goods.

"So that's the place our supplies come from," laughed Bill. "I'll see it in my mind every time I send off an order—that little man scratching through the stock hunting five hundred black-backs and three hundred deluxe mounts!"

On the Bowery we attracted no attention. There were stranger ones abroad. But the Automat was another story.

We were as fascinated as children by the Automat. It was early and we found a secluded table where we spread our silver and unloaded our trays. Happily enjoying our food, we began to look around. The diners were gathering up their food and moving with fixed faces, into our corner! In a moment every table near us was filled and people were poking food into their faces completely unaware of what they were doing, hypnotized by this sudden appearance of characters from the last Wild Western they had seen. I wished heartily that we owned some other clothes.

Again, we fled, leaving the food half eaten upon our plates. We had recognized the fixed glint in the eyes of the crowd that meant souvenir snatching.

By late afternoon the streets were jammed. Helpless, we were swept along, seeing nothing but a jumbled sea of backs and faces. Streetcars heading toward the ferries were packed. Commuters were hurrying home. The wildest cattle stampede was as nothing before the sweating mass of humanity that came thundering down upon the ferry turnstiles. The men carried folded newspapers, upon which their eyes were fastened, not missing a single word while relentlessly they bore down upon the gate, tossed in a coin, and dashed for a boat. Everyone seemed to move from long habit, totally unconscious of his own motion, oblivious to the world around him. No need to worry about curious crowds now—not one home-goer noted our presence. We were as alone as the top of Mt. Whitney.

BURRO BILL AND ME

The ferry for Jersey City pulled away from shore and we looked back at a city of myriad fairylike spires golden in the setting sun. For the first time we saw New York in all its power, its glory, its beauty and its wonder—saw in it the hope and promise with which millions of immigrant eyes have viewed it at the end of long and sordid journeys.

++++++++++

Now that we had been to New York, there was just one thing to consider before our return to the desert. I must go to Virginia. Bill could not bring himself to embarrass my family by appearing in the lumbering ark that comprised our home. Nor could I bring myself to go by train without him, in my Western attire that attracted so much attention here in the East. The long delay in making up our minds was too much for my sister. She arrived from Pennsylvania, bearing a suitcase packed for me with a dress, hose, shoes, everything to clothe me like a civilized being.

"Bill can stay here with the animals," she decreed. "You and I are taking a train to Virginia today."

Meekly I buttoned myself into the sheer navy ensemble with the black pumps and gossamer hose that kept snagging on my roughened fingers. On my sun-dried locks, I placed the tricky little black straw that seemed as superfluous as whipped cream on good solid apple pie. I felt as Bill always said, like "a black mule in a whitewashed barn," mighty conspicuous and darned uncomfortable!

But to my relief, I found that now I melted into the crowd as inconspicuously as anyone, and for the first time since our arrival I felt relaxed in this blessed anonymity. As the train swept on through Pennsylvania, Washington, past scenes familiar to my earlier days, I could almost feel myself back—a wide-eyed innocent young nurse, waiting hopefully for the great adventures that I felt sure would one day be mine. The adventures had come—but how different from any I had dreamed!

Why, I wondered to the rhythm of the rushing wheels, had I been content to live in the crudest manner, eating the barest subsistence diet, wandering afoot across desert, plains and through vast gorges, sleeping under the stars, hobnobbing with miners, Indians, herders and and bindlestiffs?

I came to with a start as my sister touched my arm and the conductor called in an accent heavily Southern, "All-ll out. All-ll out for Williamsburg!"

I was home!

Burro Bill and Mrs. Bill in 1937.

A STRANGER
COMES HOME

The memory of Williamsburg had long lain in my mind—
Williamsburg as it was that first day we had moved there at the
beginning of the first World War. Fiercely Southern, it had resisted
change until it was but a run-down replica of the proud little
village that had housed some of the greatest men in American
history. Huge mulberry trees, twisted and gnarled by a century of
living, lined leisurely unpaved streets and shaded the doorways of
shabby peeling mansions, behind whose doors First Families lived
in genteel poverty.

Now all this was changed. Rockefeller millions had touched
the town with a golden wand and almost overnight had restored
the entire town to its splendid past in the days of Washington and
Jefferson. From the College of William and Mary at one end of the
gracious old Duke of Gloucester Street, to the old State Capitol at
the other, Williamsburg was fresh with white paint, rose brick and
restored shops and taverns. Behind white colonial doors with

shining brass knockers, the same First Families now led their gracious busy lives as paid hosts and hostesses to a stream of tourists. The entire town was now one great museum, dedicated to the memory of a glorious past, and Williamsburg was pleasurably content.

From their little bungalow on Capitol Landing Road my parents had moved to a huge rose brick house, built in the seventeenth century and restored periodically through the years to a fine state of repair. A dignified old house, set in the midst of eight grassy acres, sloping gently to the banks of the broad York River. For the first time in his life, said my father, he now had room to stretch.

Delightedly, I ran from room to room and up the beautiful curving staircase to more rooms above.

"Why, you could put three desert shacks in every one," I cried, "and the bathrooms are bigger than our Baker dugout! Even your service porch would be a palace on the desert!"

"We expected that you and Bill would have this roaming out of your systems by now," my father began. "We had hoped . . ."

Hastily, my mother changed the subject. "Why," she lamented, "didn't you bring Bill and the animals with you?"

"To tell the truth," I admitted candidly, "we were afraid we'd embarrass you lumbering down the street in that modern ark, with animals in our bed, and cow-skulls grinning at the neighbors . . ."

"Fiddlesticks!" snorted my mother, "as if I cared a hoot what the neighbors think!"

It was too late to remedy that. Bill was there and I was here. I determined to make the best of it and enjoy my visit.

270

A STRANGER COMES HOME

Save for a brother in California, we were now all at home. My brother from Richmond was up on vacation, my two sisters back from their schools. Once more I was swept into the warm rich tide of affection and pride that flowed beneath the reserved exterior of the Calkins clan. Ours was a quiet conventional family devoted to educational pursuits and my mother was a practical woman with no fuss and nonsense about her—a strong woman for a dreamer like my father to lean upon.

Only in my younger sister, Gladys, did I find a trace of the rebellion that motivated Bill. Not content to go on teaching French as it was spoken in most American schools, she had flounced off to France to live, until her accent had grown so pure that she could easily pass for provincial French. Amid the whirr of the family sewing machine and the click of mother's knitting needles, the old house rang with peals of mirth as first Gladys and then I regaled the family with our "crazy stories."

In two or three days I was talked out, and I began to cast about for something to do. My mind refused to occupy itself in the small chores of a well-ordered household. Long accustomed to struggle and hardship, I could not accept even the common comforts of life without a sense of guilt in pampering myself. As a relief, I put on my brother's old pants and shirt and went out to mow the lawn, the most strenuous task at Bigler's Landing.

Trying to recapture the past, I rummaged through dusty storerooms and found fragile memories in old georgette blouses, silken kimonos and yards of crocheting that I'd once had the patience to make for flouncy tucked petticoats. There were pictures, too, of an eager young girl, standing on tiptoe to reach the shoulder of a big ox-like character with whom she had fancied herself in love.

BURRO BILL AND ME

What a dull life she would have led with that great placid creature. Thank goodness, he had remained only a picture!

Days drifted by—hot sticky days when the bees hummed lazily over the garden patch and I spent hours soaking in the bathtub, making up for lost cleanliness. "Not that it does any good," I told my mother ruefully. "We could travel a bathless week in that dry desert air without noting a suspicion of this widely-advertised Eastern ailment—B.O."

At night the family read, knitted or listened to the radio. And at night I lay in my clean white bed, in the lovely high-ceilinged room, and thought with longing of our beds of burro-brush or greasewood, spread beneath the stars, with Bill's hard body shoved against mine, back to back. I was bitterly homesick for the scent of sage in hot sunshine—for Bill, Slats and the burros.

In my restive state reading was impossible, save for some books I found by an author new to me. In John Steinbeck I could see the young Bill, eating in the "jungles," sleeping in haystacks, developing the wiry toughness that had made him indifferent to hardship, hunger or thirst. Steinbeck, too, had trod the trail that leads to nowhere, for sheer love of the trail. On his lips were the strong shocking words that at times even I restrained myself from speaking only by stern self-control.

One day I was asked to tea and sat holding my flowered cup on my lap. "Tea," I mused silently, "is better than coffee when the water smells, or when Bill has to fish out the dead birds and wood-rats. Tea with pineapple juice is something we meant to tell people about when we came back—that can of pineapple we found in an old camp and stretched even the juice by adding it to our tea."

A STRANGER COMES HOME

Around me conversation flowed, smooth, cultivated, serene. "*Anthony Adverse*—marvelous book—Steinbeck?—stark realism—but such dreadful characters. Do you suppose such people actually exist?"

"Oh yes," I blurted, glad to be on familiar ground—and stopped dead, as I felt incredulous eyes turn my way. No, it would not do to tell these people that our trails had often overlapped the paths of the jungle bum, the Dust Bowl migrant, the flotsam and jetsam of life.

Just as he had written dozens of times, to remote mailstops of the West urging us to "give up this pioneering, settle down and make something of yourselves," now again my father begged that we make our home at Bigler's Landing and take up nursing where we had left off, as though our wanderings had been but a temporary aberration. But in my mother's calm self-reliant face, I saw that she wished but one thing for her children—that they stand alone, on their own feet, and this gave me courage to refuse once and for all the haven my father offered.

I had been home for ten days when I heard from Bill. "Hurry back," he wrote. "The burros won't eat, Chiquita mourns all the time, and Slats has cried all the hair off her eyelids. She just lies in the road and waits in complete dejection. I really think she will starve to death if you don't hurry."

Hastily, I once more donned my sister's dress and hat and caught a train to New Jersey, feeling sure that Bill was but translating his own loneliness to the animals.

Bill met me at the station in Budd Lake and hugged me so tightly that my ribs cracked. "Where's Slats?" I gasped, looking about me.

"She's in the truck—I had to carry her. She won't move."

I hurried to the truck and opened the door to our bedroom. "Come, Slats," I called and reached in to pet her once-shining black fur. She raised dull eyes to mine and I saw that around them were circles of scalded bare skin, as though washed by uncounted tears. She reached a dry listless nose to my hand and sniffed. She sniffed my new dress, the dress that belonged to my sister, and turned away.

"Bill," I cried in alarm. "This dog is dying! What have you fed her? She must be poisoned!"

Bill shook his head. We drove back to camp and I went in the little tent that Bill had set up to keep things out of the rain. Relieved, I donned my plaid shirt, comfortable blue jeans and my heavy hobnailed boots, and came out. Suddenly a furry black cyclone leaped from the truck and hurled itself upon me with a glad sobbing yelp. In my sister's unfamiliar clothes, Slats had not recognized me! Like a whirling dervish she raced around and around me, leaped into my arms, ran off and frolicked for joy, and then dashed back to my arms. She was insane with happiness, her sickness cured, and from that moment Slats began to grow hair around her eyes once more. Her weeping was over. I had come home!

Over in the pasture corner, Chiquita, too, had heard my voice and was running up and down the fence, honking insistently for me to come to her. I opened the gate and she ran to me, nuzzling me all over with her soft eager nose, frisking and romping her delight. Jack and Balboa jerked up their ears, honked a welcoming "ee-ee-aw, ee-ee-aw," and tried to push down the gate to reach me.

A STRANGER COMES HOME

Even Ishy, the coyote, was hurtling around in glad welcome, adding his baby yap-yap-yap-yap to the commotion.

What a homecoming! And what a family!

Bill at 34 in 1938.

*"Muggers," 1938, Minden, Nevada. "Made $500 with this camera.
Made price of camera in two days."*

WHERE WE BELONG

Rolling down the last steep grade of our three-thousand-mile journey, we peered eagerly for familiar landmarks. Below lay the white alkali bowl of dry Soda Lake, rimmed by brown buttes and the soft blue of more distant ranges. That blue peak to the north was Avawatz, guardian of Death Valley. Over its summit, the jagged Panamints pierced the sky—the loved Panamints whose every wrinkle we knew by heart. Still farther on, the purple Argus, hidden from sight, stood sentinel over Darwin, home of our erstwhile Ford and Charlie Sam. What a world her burros had opened to us—a world unguessed by travelers in cars.

This desert scene, barren, dull to tourist eyes, was alive with memories, changing with every mile. The yucca trees with their little patch of noonday shade—how often had we rested with only our heads in that tiny shadow; glossy green of greasewood bushes—greasewood for making a healing salve, and for quick hot fuel for a cup of tea; stiff gray burro-brush, feed for our burros, springy beds for ourselves; that thin line of tender green against bare brown hill, signal of water in some canyon above. Underfoot was the warm clean sand, unsoiled by human dust, and over all the clear blue sky, unchanged since time began. Wind, sand and sun! No longer against us, but of us, and we of them!

As if reading my thoughts, Bill spoke from deep in his heart, "What more can a man desire? In this place a man can find his God."

This was the answer—the answer to all those who a thousand times had asked querulously, "Whatever do you *see* in such a life?" It was the answer to my father who wished for us security, for only in one's self does true security lie. When one has found that inner peace, that deep awareness of his own strength, he is secure in his own heart forever.

Thus ran my thoughts as the truck carried us down the long grade into Baker. We were nearing home. The white stucco of Failing's Cafe flashed in the last sunshine. To the rear, shadowy tents and shacks took form, and there was the broken line of the dry river bed, where lay our little dugout. The sun dropped slowly behind a small black butte, sending long shafts of golden light to linger on distant peaks. Out of the stillness came the chug-chug-chug of desert light plants laboring into action. One by one, all over Baker, lights winked on and overhead, one by one, the stars winked back.

Again Betty met us, big warm-hearted voluble Betty, of Dad's Tourist Cabins.

"Well, so you're back," she called cheerily. "Must have had a good season, got you a truck I see. Where you been?"

"Virginia, New Jersey, New York," grinned Bill.

"My sakes alive, New York!" ejaculated Betty. "Edna, you just tag after that Bill a few more years, and you'll wind up in some

278

poorhouse sure as you're born. Don't you know you'll never have anything, roaming around like that?"

"I have everything," I smiled, "everything that really matters."

"Well, here's some mail that came for you," said Betty, handing over a smudgy envelope, addressed in a scrawling childish hand. Bill tore it open and read, chuckling to himself.

"Well," he remarked, "guess we got more out of our trade than poor old Charlie Sam did. Listen.

" 'Burro Bill,

Ford no good. Him broke down. Tires all gone. Bring me back my burros.

Charlie Sam' "

THE END

Map Depicting
Prices' Burro Trip

North

Scale:

0	20	40

80 miles

Kings
Canyon
National
Park

NEVADA

Death Valley
National
Monument

Sequoia
National
Park

Las Ve

CALIFORNIA

Bakersfield

Baker

Barstow